# ANNULMENT

# ANNULMENT:

## Do You Have a Case?

TERENCE E. TIERNEY, JCL

SECOND EDITION

Revised and Updated by
### REV. JOSEPH J. CAMPO, JCL
Metropolitan Tribunal, Archdiocese of New York

ALBA · HOUSE    NEW · YORK
SOCIETY OF ST. PAUL, 2187 VICTORY BLVD., STATEN ISLAND, NY 10314

ST PAULS

Library of Congress Cataloging-in-Publication Data

Tierney, Terence E.
    Annulment: do you have a case? / Terence E. Tierney. — 2nd ed. /
revised and updated by Joseph J. Campo.
      p. cm.
    Includes bibliographical references.
    ISBN 0-8189-0667-7
    1. Marriage—Annulment (Canon law). I. Campo, Joseph J. II. Title.
    LAW
    262.9'.33                           93-7090
                                         CIP

Nihil Obstat:
Joseph Penna, JCD
Censor Librorum

Imprimatur:
✠ Patrick Sheridan, DD
Vicar General, Archdiocese of New York
March 22, 1993

The Nihil Obstat and Imprimatur are official declarations that a book
or pamphlet is free of doctrinal or moral error. No implication is contained
therein that those who have granted the Nihil Obstat and Imprimatur
agree with the contents, opinions or statements expressed.

Produced and designed in the United States of America by the
Fathers and Brothers of the Society of St. Paul,
2187 Victory Boulevard, Staten Island, New York 10314-6603
as part of their communications apostolate.

ISBN: 0-8189-0667-7

**Printing Information:**

| Current Printing - first digit | | 3 | 4 | 5 | 6 | 7 | 8 | 9 | 10 |
|---|---|---|---|---|---|---|---|---|---|

Year of Current Printing - first year shown

| 2000 | 2001 | 2002 | 2003 | 2004 | 2005 | 2006 | 2007 | 2008 | 2009 |
|---|---|---|---|---|---|---|---|---|---|

# CONTENTS

# PREFACE TO THE FIRST EDITION

When I was pondering the idea for this book, I conceived it as a useful tool as well as an informational manuscript.

It struck me as odd that no one had previously attempted to place into the hands of the general public a book treating of marriage annulments. I understood that no churchmen would want to go on record or in any way be accused of supporting marital failure or encouraging marriage dissolutions. At the same time, Canon Law does make provisions for annulments when individuals are found to be deserving of them. It seemed to me that what was needed was an approach which, rather than seeming to support marital breakup, actually assisted in ecclesiastical reconciliation. What was needed, I reasoned, was a useful book which would explain what annulment is, how a tribunal operates, where to go for assistance, what grounds exist for an annulment.

As you can see, the book is informational, providing the reader with a glimpse into a heretofore little known area in Church life. As a tool, the book affords both lay persons and clergy with a working guideline for the proper presentation of a case. The sad fact has been that most people in the Church are not aware of the developments which have taken place in Church Law that allow many more cases for annulment to be processed. This even extends to clergymen who have been hard pressed to keep abreast of the vast changes which have taken place in every area of Church life since the Vatican Council. Owing to this fact, many cases which deserve treatment never reach the Church court (tribunal). Thus, almost everyone is in need of some type of general information on how to proceed with a case for annulment.

An annulment is a Church declaration which states that the "marriage" in question, because of some defect, was never actually a marriage as understood by Church Law. Therefore, the Church decrees the persons free to marry. The purpose of this book is to spark readers into taking their cases to a tribunal and giving them and their parish priest some idea of what to expect from the Church court. Simply because a case is introduced does not mean the marriage will be annulled. Each marriage case must be judged on its own merits and the necessary proofs must be exhibited.

This book is not intended to spark false hopes, but the reality today is that most of the cases accepted by the tribunal for process obtain favorable resolution. Therefore, the only way anyone will know for certain the status of their marriage in Church Law is to present their case. Some do not win. But no one wins who does not apply.

It is my fondest hope that everyone reading this manuscript will be inspired to help themselves and others to straighten out their lives and at length find happiness and peace.

ANNULMENT

# Chapter One

# THE TRIBUNAL

## 1. INTRODUCTORY COMMENTS ON MARRIAGE ILLS

It is one of the great assets of personhood that people in difficult physical, mental, or emotional situations tend to remain steadfast, to stick it out, to hang on, or in current jargon "to keep on hanging on." In no situation is this virtue of steadfastness more in evidence than in the troubled marriage. It usually requires little effort to sense that something has gone awry in your marriage. Frequently, only a visceral feeling that there are problems is the indicator. You search in vain for rational standards by which to judge the degree of illness affecting your conjugal life, but to no avail.

Most people would rather discount the trouble than deal effectively with the growing suspicion that something radically wrong with their marriage is lurking in the wings. A typical flight from reality ensues and, while reason suggests a problem to be addressed, the emotions strain for flimsy excuses not to stare down those burgeoning disasters. It is not uncommon for the uneasy spouse to take the position: "I'm getting all upset over nothing when I should just let sleeping dogs lie. Perhaps it's me anyway. If I simply ignore these feelings, I'll be better off. I'm too emotional about it all."

Today, across the globe, this scene is all too frequently repeated. People sense trouble but, unwilling to admit to a problem, they deny it. The process remarkably resembles the mental and emotional stages of the terminally ill, which have been so powerfully identified and documented by Elizabeth Kübler-Ross in her book, *On Death and Dying.*

Yet, in a curious way, it shouldn't surprise us that the death of the body and the death of a marriage exhibit amazing parallels. Just as a man or woman will refuse, oftentimes vociferously, to believe they are dying, many terminal marriages find the partners just as vocally denying the possibility of real emotional trauma. But alas, as with those suffering the loss of a life which has been so precious to them, so do the partners in a conjugal misfortune have to suffer the acknowledgment of a hopeless situation and prepare, as do the dying, for the inevitable. What becomes uppermost in their minds is how can the break be cushioned so that pain can at least be diminished.

Some people are more fortunate than others. They possess a greater capacity for insightful reflection. They recognize, at an early stage in their married life, that their union is meaningless and, in a word, "terminal." Others stick it out and hang on until all the beauty, life, patience and kindness are washed out of their hearts. The breakup is inevitable but, by the time it actually occurs, the two parties to the marital misfortune are cynical and embittered. That which should have been the source of their joy and happiness ends by spawning anger and hatred, truly a sad and pitiful situation to any rational and sensitive observer. The subsequent question confronting the parties to the breakup is who can help them adjust to the aftermath of the mental and emotional turmoil which always attends such an unfortunate experience.

Lest anyone misunderstand these remarks, let it be noted that one does not desire to create the impression that marriage is a temporary commitment, easily entered into without forethought and quickly dissolved at the first sign of marital trouble. Nothing could be further from the truth. The ability to see difficult days through to a happy conclusion is admirable and an unsung virtue in today's tortured world. Married life is a wonderful, serious, yet difficult vocation. It requires commitment. It requires faith. As Pope John Paul wrote: "The Church is deeply convinced that only by the acceptance of the Gospel are the hopes that man legitimately places in marriage and in the family capable of being fulfilled" (Cf. John Paul II, Apos. Exhort., *Familiaris Consortio*, 12/15/81, #3).

An alarming number of married people discover themselves "on the rocks" simply because individuals refuse to care enough to try to resolve their difficulties. This is indeed a most regrettable situation and should be deplored. It is not to the valid marriage which has broken up due to a thoughtless and careless relationship, nor to those divorced from true sacramental unions whose own selfishness and cruelty led to their demise that we address our remarks, but rather to those conjugal irregularities and eventual breakups which were unavoidable due to the terminal character of the very marital consent. These unions were doomed, so to speak, from the outset owing to the slipshod preparation and personal defects which prevented a valid sacramental union from arising.

The Catholic Church stands alone on the mountain top, declaring the true beauty of marriage as a sacrament of divine love. Our great Church will never compromise on the indissoluble character of sacramental marriage, just as it refuses to cave into its cynical critics in other crucial matters of belief. Church law speaks specifically of two "essential properties" of marriage. One is *unity*. The other is *indissolubility* (canon 1056). Marriage has been intended by God to be a relationship between one man and one woman, and it is meant to last "until death." When all the voices of doom have long since been silenced, the Church will remain still, the most articulate advocate of love and life as it finds expression in the marriage covenant. Make no mistake about it — the Church is not in the business of running a divorce mill. Her tribunals are for justice, not deception. It was God's pastoral providence and care which led the Church to develop a system of justice for those in intolerable conjugal difficulties.

3

When other societies were developing yet easier ways to terminate a marriage the Church was engaged, through its theological, scriptural, and canonical advisors, in the process of making the justice of God more available to deserving couples. To be sure, the tribunal system has suffered occasionally from grave abuses, from both right and left wing canonists and bishops, but after taking all this into account, we must affirm that the system generally works justly and more and more people are being helped to re-enter the full sacramental life of the Church as a result of its efforts.

## 2. WHAT IS A TRIBUNAL?

You may say, "I've heard a lot lately about the good work accomplished by the Church courts in their efforts to assist broken marriages, but what is a tribunal?"

First of all, a Church tribunal is a legal forum directed by a group of judges and governed by detailed and exacting procedural laws. The judges are usually priests but, in the 1983 Code of Church Law, deacons, lay men and lay women can be named as judges by the bishop if these persons are qualified both academically and in terms of their experience in this ministry. A judge examines petitions for causes. Most of these causes are, in fact, marriage causes. Just as in civil court, a judge "hears" a case. He questions witnesses. He examines evidence. He reads the arguments of advocates. Then the judge must apply the appropriate canon law to the question at hand and render a decision.

In the case of marriage, the decision will be either that the union was null and void and therefore the parties are free to marry in the Church or have a second marriage convalidated, or that the marriage must, in good conscience, be held to be a true and valid marriage and therefore a declaration of nullity cannot be granted. It is not an arbitrary process. The judges and other staff members must follow both procedural law and the proper jurisprudence (the interpretation of the law) as handed on from Rome. They truly attempt to process a marriage case as quickly as time, manpower, and facilities will allow.

There is usually a fee for services attached, just as with a civil court, but this is generally minimal in relation to the divorce expense. The money is not kept by the priests or staff personally. It goes into diocesan funds to defray the expense of the annulment proceedings. The purpose of the fee is to cover costs, not to make money.

In spite of stories you might have heard, *no one* has been, nor ever will be, denied an annulment process because of inability to pay the court expenses. For those unable to afford the cost, the fee is waived.

## 3. APPROACHING THE PARISH PRIEST

In many dioceses, before a case gets to the tribunal, the person who is interested in a possible declaration of nullity first visits his or her parish priest or some priest counselor or friend. In other dioceses this initial interview takes place at the tribunal itself. The purpose of this initial interview is to meet with someone who will assist him or her in petitioning the tribunal for a hearing. From this point on most of the investigation is turned over to the diocesan tribunal.

Before we take a searching look at how those reading this book must evaluate their marital misfortune or perhaps assist a friend or family member to seek tribunal litigation, let us address the initial step of approaching a priest about the matter.

Not a week goes by at most rectories without the doorbell or telephone ringing at least once, bringing in its wake a tale of sadness and disillusionment over a broken marriage. The priest listens patiently to the story of heartbreak and shattered promises. He reaches into his heart for meaningful words of consolation while he struggles at the same time to offer sound, rational advice. The empathy comes easily; the advice flows with greater difficulty. The priest is there to help you, so, by all means, seek his advice and profit from his counsel. Let him assist you in petitioning for a tribunal hearing.

There was a time when the party to a broken marriage, after pouring his or her heart out to the parish priest, could expect to be met with words like these: "I know how difficult it is for you, but you simply must attempt to get back together. God wants you to persevere. There is nothing left to do. The Church can't help you." They were almost certainly well-intentioned words and may have reflected the mentality of the times, but today such a response would be considered, at the very least, ill-chosen and, at best, uninformed. Anyone who might be met with such advice today or hear words such as, "I'm sorry, I don't think you have a case," would be wise to call the tribunal in their diocese themselves. Remember, it is *not* up to the local priest to make the decision in your case. That decision devolves upon the competently trained members of the tribunal. So do not hesitate to use the means which the Church has made available to you.

## 4. HOW DOES A TRIBUNAL OPERATE?

The word "tribunal" at first glance evokes a cold, perhaps fearful, meaning and response. It sounds so formal and mechanical that one hardly considers it a pastoral organ of the Church. But the tribunal, apart from the coldness of its name, is actually a welcome friend for those caught in marital breakdown. It is *not* a place where marriage counseling takes place. It *is* a place where broken marriages and shattered lives are healed in accord with the Church's law. It is a judicial forum in which grievances are considered and rights vindicated. Presently most diocesan tribunals deal almost exclusively with marriage annulments. It is a court in which those who have "lost" in marriage may find relief from the stigma of living "outside" the Church's law.

First of all, the tribunal receives petitions for annulments from the baptized (from persons baptized or received into the Catholic Church or from a validly baptized member of another *Christian* community). They can also receive petitions for annulments from a non-baptized person. Of course, when a non-Catholic asks to have his or her marriage to be declared null, the reason is that he or she wants to enter a new union with a Catholic. The broken marriage of any two non-Catholics must be annulled or dissolved by a Petrine or Pauline Privilege before they are free to marry Catholics in the Church.

These petitions follow a somewhat legal format determined by Church Law and frequently take the form of detailed questionnaires sent to a party, usually through the medium of the parish priest. Once filled out, the petition for annulment is forwarded to the tribunal and it is there that a judgment is made on the basis of the petition as to whether or not a legitimate case for nullity exists. Therefore, *always be very detailed in your responses.*

In practice today the tribunal accepts over 90% of the petitions forwarded to it and usually proceeds to a decision. The 1983 Code is very specific in listing the situations when a petition cannot be accepted (canon 1505). There are times, however, when no valid case for nullity can be ascertained from either your petition or from a preliminary interview. This happens rarely, but it does happen, so let's not kid ourselves. Yet, happily, statistics today indicate that if you are involved in a divorce/re-marriage situation, most of the time the tribunal will assist you in rectifying your situation.

The tribunal then proceeds to call you in for an interview. Your former spouse is informed of your request for a Church annulment. Your former spouse is also requested to give his or her view and recollections regarding the problems in the relationship. This is *never* done in a confrontational manner, with the two of you present and opposing one another. The Church is not interested in who is at fault — just in the search for the truth, a search which, hopefully for you, will lead to a favorable decision. So have no fear if your former spouse decides to denounce you, or even blame you. Even if you are the guilty party, the Church is interested only in the truth and so the above situation poses no liability for your case.

Happily today, even when the respondent (the other party to this marriage) refuses to cooperate, your case can proceed — usually with the requirement of further proofs. This may be easier than it might sound. Please keep in mind: you do not need the permission of your former spouse to present a case. He or she has no power to prevent your case from being heard. But please keep in mind as well that your former spouse does have a right to be heard too. This is most important: Church law specifies that, even were a marriage annulment granted to a person, *if* for some reason the former spouse was not given the opportunity to present his or her viewpoint, the entire annulment process would be considered meaningless and without any value. The annulment itself would be "null" (canon 1620, 7°).

After each side of the case has been heard and all the facts and proofs are in, then the judge decides on the basis of the evidence whether or not the marriage in question was null and void from the beginning. There is no need to go into Church laws and jurisprudence on what constitutes a valid and invalid marriage here. Leave that complex issue for the judge to decide. It is enough for you to know that such a process exists and that the Church has expanded and is expanding the grounds for annulment through a developing jurisprudence. The picture is simple: the tribunal is a legal forum, staffed by competent personnel trained in the Church's law, and available to you if you are the unfortunate participant in a marital failure.

## 5. THE TRIBUNAL AS PASTORAL MINISTRY: AN ESSAY

One of the more exacting, yet intensely *pastoral* agencies within a diocese is the diocesan tribunal. The word "diocesan" is used here, since a tribunal is not strictly or exclusively, even though it is principally, a marriage tribunal.

Each day the staff of a diocesan tribunal is presented with cases treating the broken lives and unrequited love that is the experience of far too many couples. While individual problems are dealt with in case form, nowhere is this viewed as merely an exercise in ecclesiastical jurisprudence. That marriage cases are the subject of the Church's judicial process in no way narrows the handling of cases to pure jurisprudence. Rather, these couples represent to the tribunal judges persons who have suffered a great deal and probably for a long period of time and are now looking for healing and reconciliation in one of many forums.

Rarely has the Roman Catholic Church been in such an advantageous position to act in the manner of Jesus than when it exercises its healing ministry in cases of marital difficulty. One such avenue of reconciliation is provided by the diocesan tribunal. Due in large measure to the expanding list of justifiable factors regarding *grounds* for possible marriage annulment, tribunals have had the wherewithal, in law, for the past several decades to address many, many cases in just such a healing way.

Moreover Rome has seen fit to establish measures which will make the work of the tribunal far more expeditious than ever. Back in the early 1970's, Pope Paul VI granted to the Church in the United States special procedural norms that began to streamline the process. Such procedures were also extended, sometimes with alterations, to other countries and then to the universal Church in a document entitled *Causas Matrimoniales*. The 1983 Code of Canon Law incorporated these changes and refined them even further.

A growing and vexing problem encountered by local diocesan courts is that the more competent they become, the more cases seem to come their way. The more people they assist, the more people they discover in need of assistance. The more expeditiously the court handles cases, the greater the number of cases to challenge its efficiency. Sooner or later most competent tribunals become backlogged and eventually people suffer as a result. Generally this is a problem which can be lived with, provided that the work of reconciliation continues to encourage the people of God to avail themselves of this ministry of mercy and justice accorded them at the level of grace-filled jurisprudence.

In the past, Church tribunals always considered their efforts to judge, to the extent that this is humanly possible, whether or not a marriage was valid and sacramental an exercise in justice tempered with mercy. They may not have always considered their work as part of the Church's pastoral ministry. Today their perspective is much broader and far more sensitive to this aspect of their labors.

## HEALING JUSTICE AND MERCY

It is due to this expanded self-understanding that the Church now imbues its formal procedures with genuine healing mercy and concrete human compassion. As the Church ministers in this manner through its tribunals, it concretizes what the Lord came to do, namely, the work of reconciliation. As the author to the Letter to the Hebrews tells us, "the priest is able to deal patiently with those who have gone astray through ignorance, since he himself is subject to human weakness" (Heb 5:2).

Many of those seeking the tribunal's assistance have been the victims of cruelty and indifference and lack of love. Others have been the victims of their own selfishness, causing their spouses untold suffering. Many of those who come have been terribly hurt; others have been the cause of inexcusable ill-treatment. The diocesan tribunal is not a forum for the canonization of one or the other spouse. The Church tries to minister to both and to apply the healing grace of the Holy Spirit to saint and sinner, wounded and wounder alike. Because it seeks to imitate the Lord, it is no respecter of persons. All are offered the formal assistance of the Spirit.

Some have claimed that justice is the expression of the minimum amount of love, the least that one can expect. To offer a person justice is the barest application of the healing charity of God. The Lord left us a memorial of the love which he bore each one of us and told us that we were to love one another in just the same way. How far beyond the requirements of justice we are willing to go will indicate our commitment to the Gospel. The diocesan tribunal attempts in its efforts, not only to establish justice, but also to show mercy and witness to love. At times the harsh words of Jesus may be needed to provide a gentle correction. Other times might see the necessity for encouragement and support as innocence is clearly in evidence. Moral certitude as to the marriage's nullity may be possible, but not legally ascertained. Often one knows that a marriage is dead and believes (sometimes very strongly) that there was never a real union of life and love, but has little evidence to support that belief. The tribunal structure is good but imperfect because its judges are always dealing with intangibles and with a supra-reality which forever remains inscrutable.

## RECONCILIATION

Diocesan tribunals seek to offer a measure of reconciliation. It is to this purpose that the tribunal is dedicated and directed. Its work is a pastoral ministry in the fullest possible sense of the term because it tries to bring wholeness to the spirit of suffering human beings. At the same time it has to be admitted that, once a case is introduced into the Church court, it is exceptionally rare for the parties to reconcile. The reconciliation which is usually effected is a reconciliation with God and with the Church, a renewal of faith and hope in the lives of those who have been traumatized by an unfortunate union.

The need to be at peace constitutes the essential reason for the introduction of a marriage case in the first place. Since believers understand that the Church reflects the mind of God in matters of faith, they approach the diocesan tribunal to be reconciled with the Lord of their lives by settling accounts with the Church.

Ministering to these good people at such a time is an extremely taxing ministry. It is always hard to listen daily to the tales of broken promises, misspent energy, and shattered dreams. The tears and anxiety, so characteristic of most cases, only go to point out the fragility of human life and the need for Christian empathy. Many are the cases presented which require painful inquiry and precise responses. There is no easy way to be reconciled. The two-edged sword of truth cuts deeply as it seeks to excise the cause of pain.

The mission of the diocesan tribunal, however, has always been fruitful, even if not completely effective, for the greater majority. One reason advanced for the successful healing of many marriage cases lies with the cooperation always accorded the tribunal by those working on the parish level. Through the local priest a case is usually introduced and, after its successful completion, it is the local clergy who continue this ministry of reconciliation by drawing those involved into an ever closer contact with Christ in the Eucharist. Expertise is requisite for successful and just results, but it is the parish clergy to whom the application of healing grace has been given as their parishioners strive to remake a new life for themselves both at home with family and at home with God and His Church.

CHAPTER TWO

# EXAMINING YOUR MARRIAGE

Examining your marriage for possible signs of invalidity is certainly not a simple task, but it may not be as difficult as one might first imagine. In recent years those who have had to learn the jurisprudence of the Church and prepare for the ministry in the tribunal have been exposed to many of the fundamental criteria that are used. Several works have been composed. I believe that any serious person can engage in a searching evaluation of the marriage in question. For the purpose of such an analogy we look to a recognized expert in the field of Church Law regarding marriage to supply us with some of the necessary informational guidelines to arrive at an enlightened and, hopefully, accurate judgment. Please understand that these are not the only criteria to be used, nor would every canonist necessarily judge them to be the best. They do, however, provide food for thought and reflection.

In the 1970's Canadian Father Germain Lesage, O.M.I., who taught Canon Law at the University of St. Paul in Ottawa, proposed several concrete examples of elements which he felt were essential to a community of conjugal life and to which each marriage partner had a right. The absence of any number of these matrimonial components to a vital degree would deprive the partner of an essential right of marriage and, in terms of jurisprudence, might call the validity of the union into question.

At this juncture, we propose to take each of the elements advanced by Father Lesage and attempt to enable those reading this

13

book to apply them to their particular conjugal difficulties. Examining your marriage in terms of these criteria may assist you in forming a reasonable opinion as to the possible signs of invalidity lurking within your marriage. After this procedure is followed, the next step will be to see in which category of nullity your marital situation might fall. The concluding stage will be to ascertain what proofs will be necessary in order to prove your case before a diocesan tribunal.

How does your broken marriage measure up to these elements which Father Lesage points out as necessary for a community of conjugal life?

## 1. OBLATORY LOVE, WHICH IS NOT SIMPLY EGOISTIC SATISFACTION, BUT WHICH PROVIDES FOR THE WELFARE AND HAPPINESS OF THE PARTNER.

The "love" spoken of here constitutes an interpersonal sharing of mind, heart, and body, with a view to a growth of personality. It is not a self-serving approach to life or to the marriage itself, but a higher communication of the heart which always cares for and looks to the needs of the beloved. Through a conscious effort to supply for the other's needs and the promotion of a mutual self-fulfillment which brings happiness to both parties, a union of life and heart arises which is a sign of the graced nature of married life. This mutual blending of lives constitutes a sign of God's Kingdom and establishes the community of life and love which characterizes the sacrament of marriage.

Many people have a faulty understanding of what marital love is all about. The bond of marriage arises when, in a moment of grace, two people give themselves to each other for life through an act of consent. Since one can hardly be expected to consent to a union which would be destructive, marriage requires that the parties who give themselves to each other be able to provide the love and sharing that is at least minimally necessary for a blending of hearts. When the marriage consent, once exchanged, is selfless—that is, when each party places the partner's needs at the top of their list of priorities—only then can we speak of "oblatory love" within the union.

Marriage "in the Lord," a reality of which St. Paul speaks so eloquently, must be grounded on living faith. This mutual faith in God ought then to become the cornerstone to the marriage. It is the spiritual reality of grace and faith which is the foundation for a true sacramental marriage. Where faith is lacking, love will be diminished. If love is diminished, the mutual blending of lives cannot be adequately realized. If this *faith-love* is not present, either at the time of the wedding ceremony or is not supplied thereafter, one can reasonably assume that the spiritual foundation for Christian marriage is lacking. Ask yourself:

— Was my marriage with _____ really a mutual blending of lives? Did we share our minds and hearts unselfishly?

— Was a deep faith in God characteristic of our union?

— Did we seek to adequately provide for each other's needs? Was one or both of us self-serving, thinking only of self first and only secondarily attempting to be a loving partner?

— How strongly did we communicate with each other and share in the grace of marital love which never seeks to be wholly self-centered?

— Did we seek to provide mutual fulfillment in our marriage? Were either or both of us more concerned with self-fulfillment as a person to the diminishment of the other?

— How strongly did we try or were we able to maximize one another's potential to grow? Perhaps one of us held the other back from true growth of personality simply because of jealousy.

— Were either of us unusually jealous? Why?

— As love produces happiness, were we happy and did we enjoy one another's talents and gifts? Did we share our talents?

— Read over in your Bible chapter 13 of St. Paul's First Letter to the Corinthians. Did your marriage possess the quality of love spoken of so beautifully by Paul?

— Use the definition of love contained in that chapter. How did you and your partner measure up to the *true* nature of love as described by St. Paul?

— Examine each and every line and apply it to your experience of marriage. Then reflect upon it prayerfully and ask yourself, "How did we measure up?"

— Finally, ask yourself this one last question: "Did we honestly exchange in our consent the same kind of love described by St. Paul?"

Having done this, proceed to evaluate your answers as objectively as possible. Remember, honesty cannot be compromised. Which of you were more at fault? Did you share equally in this selfishness?

## 2. RESPECT FOR CONJUGAL MORALITY AND FOR THE PARTNER'S CONSCIENCE IN SEXUAL RELATIONS.

As anyone involved in the matrimonial court will readily admit, sexual difficulties in marriage take a large share in the subject matter of many cases introduced for resolution. We are not referring here solely to those cases involving sexual abnormalities or aberrations, but also to marriage breakdown which involves sexual difficulties of any sort whatsoever. Sooner or later, in one way or another, sexual tension and problems surface in most marital irregularities whether these difficulties be a *cause* or an *effect* of the marital discord.

The reason sexual relationships suffer in most marriages of

questionable validity (to be sure, valid marriages often endure some measure of difficulty in this area too; however, resolution can be forthcoming largely as a result of the sacramental love between the marriage partners) is due to the fact that the sexual dimension of shared matrimonial love forms the highest degree of that sharing. Since sexual love is at the core of true conjugal love, any sexual tension can indicate a problem, more or less deep-seated. Lest one be tempted to misconstrue these remarks, be assured that in no way should you conclude that sexual problems always indicate the invalidity of a marriage. Clearly this is not the case. However it should be noted that many invalid marriages do have some sexual problem as its cause. More importantly, tumultuous sexual problems often point to another recognized ground for annulment or indicate the absence of shared conjugal love. Needless to say, any examination of marriage with a view to establishing a case for invalidity must take a searching look into the sexual dimension of the marriage union in question.

In marriage, if a person truly loves the other, he or she evidences an abiding respect for the partner's conscience in matters that are sexual. When this conjugal respect in the sexual area of married life is absent or defective, then one can reasonably presume that the matrimonial love itself is absent or defective.

What constitutes lack of sexual respect? First of all, in the area of birth control, refusal to respect the conscience of the other concerning the means used to regulate the size of one's family can indicate a serious defect in conjugal love. Frequently artificial means of birth control are practiced as a means of avoiding the procreation of children *completely*. This would constitute certain invalidity. Did one partner have a hidden agenda about being open to the new life which is a normal fruit of the conjugal act? A particular married couple could find themselves torn over this very significant and crucial marital component. Did the marriage occur directly because one person, by means of deceit, had his or her own fixed attitude regarding these matters and withheld that information precisely because such a revelation would have led to a breakup prior to the wedding? Such a withholding of information shows a lack of respect which (given what was evidently a deep division between them over so serious a matter) might reveal that the consent exchanged at the time of the wedding ceremony was faulty to begin with, and thus invalid.

Occasionally one party will force sexual intercourse upon the other, thus destroying the very meaning of sexual love. Or they may insist on practices which degrade or disgust the partner. Today oral sex is often engaged in as a means of sexual expression. What happens when one party finds this act "dirty," revolting, and immoral, but the other partner insists that such acts be performed? What happens when oral sex becomes a hidden means to prevent conception? This type of thing can be indicative of a deep disrespect for a person's conscience and morality. The forced violation of another's conscience is a very serious example of utter selfishness. In fact, the entire area of marital sexuality is a clear barometer of the degree of selfishness within a conjugal union. The presence of selfishness to a profound, serious and consistent degree raises legitimate questions regarding a person's capacity for marriage, and thus the matter of a marriage's very validity is brought into question. Ask yourself:

— To what degree was your sexual relationship truly a joining of mind and heart, body and spirit?
— If it was "unfulfilling," what does that mean? And why was it so?
— Was there gross selfishness involved in your sexual relationship? If so, on whose part?
— Did this selfishness surface in other areas of your married life?
— Did either of you force the other to engage in abnormal sexual acts?
— Just how was the question of birth control or contraception dealt with? Was this a major problem? How did you both react and solve this issue?

## 3. RESPECT FOR THE HETEROSEXUAL PERSONALITY OR "SENSITIVITY" OF THE MARRIAGE PARTNER.

At first reading one would be inclined to conclude that this section treats of homosexuality in marriage. While this rather complex marital configuration will be discussed in greater length at another point, for the moment we will limit our remarks to the following observations. Those who work in the tribunal learn that homosexuality in marriage is not uncommon. It has been my own experience that homosexuals frequently marry members of the opposite sex. They do so for a variety of reasons. Some desire to keep their sexual orientation hidden from family, friends, business associates, etc. Still others have conflicting sexual drives which cause them to relate physically to members of both sexes. The fact of their homosexual activity places such so-called "bisexual" persons within the "homophile" category. Some homosexuals, and these are admittedly rare cases, come to recognize their homosexuality only upon entering a marital relationship which demands heterosexual activity and sharing. Once confronted with the prospect of sharing physically with someone of the opposite sex, they are forced to take a hard look at themselves and acknowledge their situation. Whatever the motivation behind marrying, homosexuality is one of the categories of severe problems which may lead to a judgment by the Church that a marriage must be rendered null and void. If your marriage falls into this category, consult with your diocesan tribunal. You probably have a case for annulment.

The primary thrust of our discussion here, though, will center on the respect one partner ought to have for the other based upon their sexual identity as male or female. For our purposes, "heterosexuality" applies to the *respect* that a man should have for a woman as woman, and the reciprocal respect a woman should have for a man as man. This respect translates into a sensitivity for the unique personal sexual difference between the sexes. A man tends to approach marriage and other things in one way, with a particular "male" outlook and perspective. A woman, on the other hand, tends to look at marriage from a decidedly different perspective. In our age and culture, which seems to take offense at the thought of male and female as being "different" in these ways, I assure you that any judge in a tribunal learns of these vastly different perspectives after merely a week or two of listening to testimony. In a truly loving conjugal relationship, both man and woman understand and respect the different mental and emotional approaches to married life that accompanies their sexual identity.

For example, a man will view certain marital problems in one way and a woman will look at the same difficulties in yet another manner. The woman will shoulder emotional pressures in a manner markedly distinct from the way a man might handle the same pressures. What personal touches the female personality requires for emotional happiness and marital integration will not be found in the male counterpart. His personality will require distinctly different personal touches. Thoughtfulness displayed, for example, in the form of cards, flowers, candlelight dinners, simple warm human touches, are treasured by the female. The thoughtfulness which a man appreciates is often of a different nature. Here are some questions to consider:

— How sensitive were you to your spouse's needs? How sensitive was your marriage partner to your own needs?
— Did your marriage display a lack of thoughtfulness to the point that the respect for the unique needs of the other led to gross insensitivity?
— Were you treated by your spouse as a person ought to be treated as a man or woman? Did you treat your spouse as a man or woman ought to be treated?

Examine your conjugal life together. If this dimension of sensitivity was shamefully absent, perhaps even graver abuses affecting the very bedrock of the marital bond itself likewise existed. If so, then your marriage was more than impoverished; it could even be null and void before God and the Church. A lack of conjugal love may well be one indication that your union possibly lacked some of the essential qualities necessary for validity. A gross personal and emotional insensitivity for the spouse's needs can be a sign of this. Has this been the experience of your married life?

## 4. RESPECTIVE RESPONSIBILITY OF BOTH HUSBAND AND WIFE IN ESTABLISHING CONJUGAL FRIENDSHIP.

You may have heard it said that husband and wife must not only be conjugally united but must also become, if they are not already, friends. The concept of *friendship* within marriage is pregnant with meaning for it is at the very heart of what married life is all about. For a marital union in the true sense of the word, you need more than a sacred ceremony and State recognition. Love, and above all, friendship is needed! For if couples cannot enjoy one another as two inseparable friends, they will not, without intolerable difficulty, make it through the years of marital turmoil which inevitably lie ahead. Only that "staying power" so characteristic of true friendship will allow the spouses to live in that bonding which was God's intent: that "two become one."

Why friendship? Friendship is basically a higher form of love than the physical expression so characteristic of marriage. We are using the term "physical" here in the sense of sexual but it should also be understood as a close living arrangement. In a word: marriage partners live in a fishbowl of physical proximity, materially and sexually. But the material and sexual cannot conceive love nor bring it to term. It is given to conjugal friendship to effect and build a loving union. Why? Because the quality of love constitutive of friendship transcends the material and sexual and rises to the heights of the spiritual. It is grace filled. If the bedrock of marriage is friendship, then impotency or sterility will have no long-term or lasting effects. Personal problems, material hardships (finances, loss of job, disappointments, difficulties with the children, etc.) will not shake a marriage to its foundation. The tremors of pain will recede for something higher is at stake. Something more lasting and precious is at the origin of your shared life.

I neither see nor feel a compelling need to enumerate for you the qualities of friendship. You are all too familiar with this from personal experience. Rather suffice it to say that without those whom you love, apart from your family and spouse, namely your friends, you could not long hope to carry on bravely in life's painful situations. Those same loving vibrations which you experience between yourself and your friends must likewise be present between you and your spouse. If they are missing, your life together is hollow; your love, sterile. This leaves questions that could perhaps touch upon the very validity of your marriage.

Nothing as important or as treasured as friendship can be built up easily. As with the inventor or artist who selflessly expends all his energy to see the realization of his dreams, so too the lover if he or she chooses to build a marriage which will last, invests his or her full energy in fashioning a loving friendship. There is *no* other way. Nothing short of this will do. Let us examine your marriage and focus for a time on the element of matrimonial friendship:

— Did both of you expend the energy required to build a loving relationship based on the Gospel love of the Christian life? Did both of you have the capacity to do so?

— Did you and your spouse work toward establishing and maintaining the necessary elements that make up a marital friendship? Did you both understand how necessary this is?

— Was the foundation of your marriage this higher form of love?

— Did both of you honestly and to the best of your ability work to your limits to sustain this love?

— Did either or both of you fail to give to the other this true loving service?

If you have had to answer negatively to many or most of these questions, then perhaps the qualities of a loving conjugal friendship were absent from your marriage. If this is the case, then an authentic question must be raised regarding the meaning and reality of what canonists call the *object of your matrimonial consent*. Just what did you give consent to? Was it marriage as the Church understands marriage? This includes the notion of conjugal friendship. Here, once again, a question regarding the validity of the marriage appears.

## 5. RESPECTIVE RESPONSIBILITY OF BOTH HUSBAND AND WIFE IN PROVIDING FOR THE MATERIAL WELFARE OF THE HOME: STABILITY IN WORK, BUDGETARY FORESIGHT, ETC.

How often tribunal officials hear these words from the mouths of petitioners and respondents alike: "That person never did a day's work in his/her life. All he/she did was jump from job to job." "He'd stay a few months, or even weeks, and either quit or get fired." "For all she cared, the house could have fallen in on us." "When he did work he spent most of the money on booze, drugs, the horses, you name it." "She was so irresponsible that you'd think she was still fourteen years old."

There are, of course, countless variations on the theme. "The house was a pigpen. She spent the day parked in front of the TV watching all those crazy soap operas and talk shows." "I'd come home from work when he would have been off. He'd have spent the whole day watching football. He was too 'busy' to take care of the kids; that was woman's work to him!" "The kids were never dressed properly, and I wonder if they ate properly either." "He never saved a penny. He was like a drunken sailor." "She was disgusting, a slovenly wife in a dirty house."

These comments present pathetic images of married life, but unhappily they very often reflect what is perceived or experienced as true. Far too many persons marry while remaining unfit to establish and maintain a home. Unconcerned for the humdrum details of married life, the "bread and butter" realities of living together, irresponsible people carry on as if their needs alone mattered. Lacking a sense of domestic responsibility, they create an unlivable marriage.

Admittedly one does not have to know how to run a "Wall Street" business to contract a valid marriage. Marriage is not reserved to the "perfectly" mature or "perfectly" responsible. But certainly some minimal degree of financial know-how ought to be expected from rational adults. Most of the complaints cited in this section are the result, not of imbecility, but certainly from at least an abnormally thoughtless, careless, self-centered kind of conduct. Since it can be assumed that a reasonable person neither would nor should give consent to a marriage in which such irresponsibility abounds, it can be deduced that if a marriage turns out to be the kind about which we have spoken, then questions regarding defective consent to the marriage ought to be raised.

There is another point as well. Such a slovenly irresponsible union may be indicative of other constitutive problems. These marks of irresponsibility may be signs of deeper, more pervasive difficulties which will surely surface upon closer examination. Quite often it will be these deeper problems that result in a decree of nullity.

— How did your marriage measure up to the demands of domestic responsibility? Were there similarities to the signs of irresponsibility described in the opening remarks of this section?

— Did either you or your spouse regularly exhibit signs of financial irresponsibility?

— Were either of you unconcerned with the details of providing a decent home for the other and all that this implies and demands?

Take a good hard look for yourself. Examine your marriage. See if perhaps your marital situation resembles the irresponsibility just outlined. If your marriage approximates this type of irresponsibility, perhaps you ought to be seeking aid and advice about the very validity of the union. Upon canonical examination, perhaps more substantive grounds will emerge (this is almost always the case) that might provide a genuine possibility for an annulment.

## 6. MORAL AND PSYCHOLOGICAL RESPONSIBILITY IN THE GENERATION OF CHILDREN.

With all the discussion surrounding the population "explosion" and "responsible" parenthood, it is little wonder that the question of begetting children causes some uneasiness. Furthermore, the contemporary social and financial circumstances of many force them to consider seriously the issue of family size so as to bring their lived marital situation into line with the demands of practical living. Couple all of this with the various breakthroughs in the field of birth control and contraception along with the media's promotion of a swinging lifestyle for singles and its calculated and concerted determination to promote the use of condoms to prevent disease and unwanted pregnancies, and you have set the stage for real confusion among our Catholic young people. For Roman Catholics who are faithful to both the letter as well as the spirit of Church teaching, the issue of family planning takes on serious moral implications as well.

Extremes of any sort are to be avoided. If virtue stands in the middle, then perhaps regarding the generation of children, married couples must set their sights on a reasonable middle ground so to make it possible for them to adequately handle God's precious gift of life to their family. This search for the middle course of action implies balance and stability; it likewise implies marital cooperation and consensus. Responsibility is the key here. Married couples have a responsibility to raise a family, providing there are no *serious* physical, psychological, or financial obstacles to this Christian goal. Their responsibility extends beyond procreation. They must provide a suitable environment for the physical, mental, moral and emotional well-being of their offspring and must see to their spiritual development as well. Canon Law never speaks of "procreation" as the sole or even the primary end of marriage. Where children are concerned it always speaks of their "procreation and education" (cf. canon 1013 #1 of the former code of Canon Law or canon 1055 #1 of the present code).

Not infrequently one stumbles upon couples who either refuse to have children or who beget a family so large that it is unmanageable both financially and psychologically. These are the extremes we alluded to before; these are the extremes to be avoided.

Both husband and wife *must* discuss their prospects for a family in an atmosphere of mutual love and sharing. If this planning is not done, then they can reasonably expect marital trouble. Only through dialogue can the couple adequately assess their needs, goals, and resources. Failure to analyze and plan together usually results in frustration, anger and even marital disaster.

Misunderstanding is frequently a byproduct of not planning. Prior to marriage, many couples (in fact probably most couples) do not communicate their desires and goals relative to family size. Therefore, once married they frequently discover that they have differing points of view on what should constitute their family. This tendency to remain non-communicative prior to marriage generally carries over into the marriage itself. This constitutes an irresponsible preparation for their future together which only spells problems down the road.

Procreating a family implies the psychological readiness to meet the demands a family will place upon a couple. It is for this reason that the Church discourages hastily entered into unions, or marriage as an afterthought following upon an extramarital pregnancy. This psychological readiness for marriage appears to be a necessary prerequisite for entering into a valid marriage in the eyes of the Church. Current decisions of many tribunals, not only here in the United States but elsewhere as well, indicate that a large number are approaching marriage nullity cases from this perspective.

Preparedness for marriage includes the ability to carry out the demands of married life. One of the "burdens and responsibilities" of marriage is the generation and care of the children to be born of the union. This forms a major aspect of marital consent as understood by the Church.

Proper sexual identification and sex roles figure prominently here. A father must become a father in the truest sense of the term and execute the role proper to him as a father. The same holds true for the mother. If a man is unable to carry out his fatherly role, in relation to his sons and daughters, he is in a sense irresponsible. A child must not come to experience a mother cast in a paternal-maternal role, nor a father acting as both mother and father. This is not merely irresponsible. It has proven to be psychologically harmful to the emotional health of the children. Inability to assume their responsible roles in the family constitutes not only gross negligence but may indicate a psychological inability to assume one of the essential obligations of marriage as well. This raises very real questions regarding possible nullity. Examine your marriage:

— Was it in any way an "irresponsible" marriage based on the foregoing observations?
— Did either of you show such signs of irresponsible behavior?
— Did pre-marital pregnancy enter into the picture at all regarding your decision to marry?
— Did you assume your proper marital roles as husband and wife, father and mother?
— Did you communicate to one another regarding a family?
— Did you have any children? If not, why not?
— Did you have more children than you could adequately and properly care for? If so, why?
— How conscientious were you both in rearing your children?

— Did you *both* plan for the education and growth of your children?

## 7. PERSONAL MATURITY AS EXPRESSED IN ONE'S DAILY CONDUCT IN THE ORDINARY EVENTS OF LIFE.

It should come as no surprise to anyone that chronological age is no sure barometer of psychological age. Simply stated: age is no sure guide to maturity. Because age gives us no absolutely certain clue to the maturity of a given individual, it is eminently possible for a person to be "old enough" to marry but not be "mature enough" to assume the obligations of a marital commitment. This situation arises frequently today with the result that many marriages are doomed from the beginning.

There are a number of classical signs that point to an immature personality. It is extremely difficult to present an exhaustive list. The problems or signs of immaturity can differ from individual to individual. There are cultural issues at stake here as well, and what is deemed acceptable at one stage of life for a male or female in a given cultural environment may well be a sign of immature behavior in another. Owing to this rather complex situation, let us simply discuss some aspects of immaturity as they relate and touch upon marriage in our society in the United States at the beginning of the third millennium.

Anyone who claims to be mature must be responsible. *Responsibility* includes the personal ability to act freely and willingly without being told what to do or being coerced into doing it by someone else. Children generally are not responsible since they must rely on others to tell them what to do and when to do it and, often, how it should be done.

A marriage partner must be able to act judiciously and reliably. They must be personally accountable for the obligations which they freely take upon themselves. They ought to evidence this with regard to marriage and family life and not have to be told what to do and when to do it. They must be persons upon whom others can depend. They must be able to provide a decent and loving home, to secure and maintain a good job with an adequate income, to plan ahead and make provisions for various options for the proper upbringing of their children. If a man or woman cannot be depended upon to fulfill these marital roles, they may truly be labeled immature. *Dependability* is a sure sign of maturity. Its opposite is a clear and certain indication of its absence.

Another aspect of maturity is *accountability*. The responsible and mature personality will be willing to stand up and answer for his or her actions and decisions. Therefore, a mature person will not be afraid to act, nor shirk his responsibility to answer for his or her movements or activities. In marriage husband and wife must provide for the needs and burdens of family life and to that extent are answerable to the family and to society for the way in which they meet those needs. If they fail to provide as they ought, they show signs of immaturity.

Married couples should conduct themselves in a manner becoming to their state in life. The attendant responsibilities must be accepted and shouldered. Nothing less will do. They may occasionally slip and fail to fulfill these responsibilities, but the overall picture of their lifestyle ought to manifest an underlying maturity.

Still another gauge for judging maturity or the lack of it is the presence of gentleness and kindness of character and manners in their mutual relationships. The truly mature personality, although not perfect in attitude or manner, at least exhibits a degree of courtly graciousness when dealing with others, especially within the context of a loving conjugal union. Even in the presence of enemies, mature persons, while perhaps given a measure of anger and frustration, conduct themselves in a basically decent manner. These persons respect another individual's rights even when they might viscerally desire to inflict bodily harm. Such dignified demeanor is but one sign of a truly integrated and mature personality.

Within the context of married life a mature and responsible individual is aware of the need for gentleness and kindly love. Whether it be on the part of the man or the woman, this type of character trait is essential to marital growth. This tender approach to the spouse signifies the loving concern one spouse should have for the other. It is not only the decent way to treat others but the crucial factor in nourishing marital love.

To be sure, there will be times of bitter disappointment with one's spouse; to be sure, domestic battles will occur; to be sure, quirks of personality will grate upon a marriage partner; to be sure couples will become annoyed with each other over matters both large and small. This is human life and no one is perfect. Perfection is not the answer; love is. However, though little things will cause flare-ups, the benefit of maturity is that it keeps the flare-ups in their proper perspective. Maturity never allows small, insignificant difficulties to become marital disasters. Reason prevails, and maturity always shows signs of *forgiveness* and *contrition*. It is this mutual understanding nurtured by a mature approach to love and life which keeps people together and growing. Treating one's spouse with kindness and understanding is a sure sign of maturity. Failure to be gentle, forgiving, understanding, and so on, is a clear warning of a lack of maturity on the part of at least one of the marriage partners.

Still another aspect of marital maturity is *"stability" of conduct* and *"adaptability" to changing circumstances.* Maturity is characterized by personal stability, which allows for the responsible handling of life's pressures, tensions, and accelerating change. In the context of marital maturity, stability refers to a responsible lifestyle which looks to insure the permanence of the marriage, that which the Catholic Church refers to as its "indissolubility." Stability and adaptability flow from maturity, from the sense of personal responsibility for the care of one's spouse and family.

Stability implies a measure of equilibrium. This notion of balance rightly defines maturity. Balance signifies a commonsense approach to problems, a rational response versus an irrational or overly emotional one. In marriage, maturity can be identified by looking to the quality of the spouses' personal stability. Can they handle the demands of family life? The answer to this is quite important, for a negative response could possibly indicate grounds for nullity.

An immature personality tends to fluctuate wildly. Predictable responses of such a person are hardly calculable. For this reason, marriage to such a person may at best be an unhappy experience. By nature all of us tend toward what we believe will bring us happiness. No reasonable person can be expected to give consent to any sort of relationship that will bring only unhappiness and pain. No rational personality desires marriage to a grossly immature person. I have often asked persons who eagerly point out the faults and obvious immaturity of their former spouse: "But why would a mature individual be attracted to someone so immature?"

Immature people lack stability. Stability is a basic quality that tends toward permanence. Permanence is what love seeks! If on any given day you must guess at whether your spouse will be kind or hostile, or likewise if your spouse has to speculate about whether you will be understanding or impossible, there is a very real question of a lack of maturity present. Admittedly anyone can have a "bad day" on occasion, but when "bad days" are frequent and unpredictable, then it becomes impossible to carry on a fulfilling or meaningful marital relationship. Exasperation follows upon frustration, and not surprisingly this can often lead to a breakup in the marriage.

Life has at the very foundation of its definition a measure of changefulness. It forever seeks growth; it craves evolution; it thrives on forward movement. This quality of changeability causes many a person a sleepless night, but it also gives birth to love. The mature person understands this principle of growth. Such a person learns to believe in the goodness of change and the beauty of creation. Because that person understands and appreciates stability, she or he adapts to those moments of change which creep into everyone's life sooner or later. They react to change not with fear, but respond to it with hope, the hope that this change in life will bring joy and peace.

None of us knows when and where the challenges of change will throw our life into a maelstrom. No one can predict the death of loved ones, the sudden onslaught of financial misfortune, the terror of terminal illness. The manner in which we handle our troubles will signify our degree of maturity. Since even the mature person is brought to the brink of collapse when confronted with one of these situations, it can be expected that the immature, when similarly confronted, will react in the same inappropriate ways by which they have already been living their lives. A good test of marital maturity is how spouses react to the changing circumstances which turn their lives upside down. The question that ought to be raised at this point is: "Was my marriage one marked by truly severe immature behavior or attitudes?" Gauge your response after careful analysis of what has just been said. Perhaps you have been involved in a grossly immature relationship. Maybe, because of this, your marriage can be declared null and void by the Church.

— Were there signs of underlying immaturity present prior to the marriage?
— If so, what were they and how deeply did these signs manifest themselves in your marriage?
— Based on the criteria discussed above, was your union characterized by sound and responsible living?
— Examine the approach taken to work, family, housekeeping, the children, neighbors, relatives and friends, vacations, and so on. Can you say that your marriage showed signs of maturity and common sense in these areas? If no, why not?
— Did one or many areas indicate more prominently the lack of a mature approach to the responsibility and demands of conjugal life?
— Could you or your spouse be depended upon?

— Did your marriage express signs of gentleness, kindness, and patience?

— Did you or your spouse treat one another in a dignified manner?

— Were signs of understanding and tenderness present in the marriage?

— Could you rely on each other for forgiveness and contrition?

— Was your spouse a stable personality?

— Were you and your spouse capable of reasonably adjusting to the changing circumstances and pressures which entered your life together?

If you are forced to respond by indicating a woeful lack of maturity in your marriage, perhaps your union was invalid. Perhaps, too, upon examination at the hands of competent tribunal personnel, even more substantive proofs or grounds of nullity may surface. This has been the experience of many involved in tribunal ministry.

One point ought to be kept in mind. There are many devout Catholics who have questioned this issue of "maturity" as an indication of a person's capacity for marriage. Many sincere and good priests have wondered if this were not just an "excuse" for what has become a Church "divorce." At the same time, it has been my personal experience that one frequently finds the most ardent opponent of Church annulments singing a different tune when it becomes a question of a problem marriage in his or her own family. One must never forget the very human dimension to our Church.

Again, with regard to this notion of maturity, an *excess* must be avoided. Back in 1979 a Judge on the Roman Rota (the Supreme Court of the Church, as it were) noted that we must not fall into the trap of making marriage the "crowning of maturity already acquired, but as a step in the process by which fuller maturity is to be attained" (cf. S.R.R., c. Pompedda, 7/3/79: RRD, vol. 71, p. 38 as quoted in *Forum: A Review of the Maltese Ecclesiastical Tribunal*, Vol. 3, 1992, No. 1, p. 103). "Maturity" as such becomes the issue before a Church court when it is realized that a given individual (or perhaps both parties for that matter) lacked even the minimal maturity that one should reasonably expect from a person of the appropriate age and mentality. One should carefully examine the marriage that has failed or is failing. Is there an authentic question to be asked whether each of the parties was capable of acting in a mature fashion? If the pattern of a person's life indicates that even with good intentions, immature and unreasonable behavior is the norm, then questions about a person possessing even that minimal level of maturity must be raised. If that is the case, then the person's very capacity for marriage is indeed an issue that should be brought before a Church court.

## 8. SELF-CONTROL OR TEMPERANCE, WHICH IS NECESSARY FOR ANY REASONABLE AND "HUMAN" FOCUS OF CONDUCT.

## 9. MASTERY OVER IRRATIONAL PASSION, IMPULSES OR INSTINCTS WHICH WOULD ENDANGER CONJUGAL LIFE AND HARMONY.

Self-indulgence and intemperance have long been a problem plaguing the human community. It did not begin with Henry VIII or Louis XIV. Lack of self-mastery is evident among all of us. Perhaps we are in need of being reminded, occasionally, that the sins of others are basically our own sins. What we denounce as despicable in another is never truly absent from ourselves. Awareness of one's own weakness and limitations is a sure step in the long and, at times arduous, process of gaining control over our human appetites.

Marriage has always suffered at the hands of self-indulgence. From the very origin of the institution that we label marriage, conjugal difficulties have arisen because couples have lost (or never developed in the first place) the virtue of temperance. Even in our highly mobile and sophisticated society we have yet to conquer the culprit which has set couples at one another's throats. The evil has several names: selfishness, intemperance, self-indulgence. Each name merely demonstrates a different side or emphasis to the same problem. Surely we cannot do away with all human error; just as surely we cannot insulate life from its sinfulness. A theological reality must be affirmed: Jesus came among us and redeemed our human nature. But He did not change it or remove its weaknesses. Even if we cannot escape the inescapable side of human life, surely we can be more discriminating when it comes to choosing a partner for life and making a decision to marry that person. This much is certain.

When we speak of intemperance or lack of self-control, we are *not* immediately referring to alcohol, drugs, or sex. To be sure, both substance abuse and abuse of the gift of human sexuality are among the prime abuses when it comes to intemperance and personal lack of self-control. These marital "beasts" form but a single dimension of abuse. One wishes at times that such problems could be so easily limited to a couple of categories. Unfortunately, life is never quite that simple.

Take, for instance, the compulsive shopper. (For our purposes here, we will use the female sex as an example, although clearly this problem is not solely a female one). She reads the evening newspaper feverishly searching for new gimmicks or instant bargains. This becomes a daily ritual. What she reads tonight will become a financial disaster tomorrow. She cannot resist the urge to buy, buy, buy. Such limited vision is what retail fortunes are made of. This problem wasn't quite so evident many decades ago when cash was the basic medium of exchange and people did their shopping on Saturdays. But with the advent of malls and supermarkets, 24-hour shopping and the use of credit cards with competitive finance charges, the intemperate shopper has emerged. How many marriages have fallen on hard times simply due to excessive and foolhardy spending.

This example of intemperance is but one form of selfishness.

Perhaps it is, on some level, a type of "psychological compensa-tion." However it is labeled, the simple truth is that such uncon-trolled, compulsive activity sooner or later pervades the whole of one's conjugal life. If you examine your marriage and the evidence of this type of approach to living is evident, perhaps there exists yet more serious reasons for the failure of your marriage.

The classical example of intemperance is alcohol. This plague (which might point to the dreaded disease of alcoholism) can be one of *the* most devastating problems to afflict a marriage. There is much talk today relative to alcoholism and its effects upon family harmony and stability. Thank God we have come to recognize alcoholism for what it is: a sickness. Hopefully one day help will be easily available for all who are affected. Great praise ought to be given to groups such as A.A. for the lives and at times the marriages that have been saved through their very demanding and spiritual "Twelve-Step Program."

But what of your marriage? Is alcohol a problem? Is it simply over-indulgence which leads to abuse and embarrassment, or is it alcoholism—the sickness? It is crucial for the purpose of an annulment that the distinction between the sickness of alcoholism and heavy drinking or classical intemperance be drawn. Alcoholism is one thing. Intemperance is quite another. Neither of them *of themselves* is listed in Church Law as specific grounds for nullity. Yet in the jurisprudence of the Church, in the many decisions of Church tribunals, both alcoholism and intemperance are seen as having possible and probable serious effects upon a person's very ability to marry. Each problem is approached from a different perspective. One may of itself, under certain conditions, render a person incapable of marriage. The other may be an indication of some other deeper problem which might be the cause of nullity.

You know as well as I that we could go on listing examples of intemperance for pages. It is enough that we are aware that lack of personal mastery and gross intemperance lead to marital troubles which work toward the breakdown of conjugal life. Perhaps in a union characterized by these two culprits a true Christian marriage never existed in the first place.

The mastery over one's life has long been a "Holy Grail" pursued doggedly by women and men throughout history. It has always been considered a blessing when couples were able to be themselves and act and live responsibly. On the other hand, it has forever been considered a curse to be one of those persons who cannot "get hold of themselves," who are unable "to pull it all together" or who fail to see the value of self-denial. To be governed and ruled by one's passions is a cruel and self-defeating way to live. Happiness becomes a dream one never attains.

— Was your marriage based upon mutuality, sharing, and selflessness, or were the opposing manifestations of the vice of selfishness the basis of your union?

— Did your marriage possess signs of irrationality or intemperance?

— If so, in what areas? (Frequently the area in question will be the issue that can affect the validity or nullity of the marriage.)

— How did the problem begin? When did it begin? Who was at fault? What role did the innocent party play in "enabling" this behavior?

— Did you or the other party suspect anything of this sort prior to marrying?

— Was one party warned by others (family members, friends, co-workers, the parish priest, etc.) about this problem, but that party refused to listen?

— How did intemperance, or lack of self-control, or irrationality, or passion affect the reasonable functioning of your life together?

Ask yourself these and other questions. If you find that your marriage was an example of this classic problem, perhaps you have a case for an annulment. Let the tribunal take a look.

## CONCLUSION

Today only brash dreamers would venture a prediction that any particular marriage will endure a lifetime. The wise are never so fooled as to conjecture regarding the future outcome of any situation involving emotional and rational creatures. The simple fact is that no one knows for certain just what elements hold one marriage together and which lead to destruction in another. Many have been the times when I have been presented with a marriage annulment case where, to the outsider, the relationship seemed destined for unending joy. They were called "the perfect couple" by anyone's standards. And yet further questioning revealed the incredible depth of sadness and abuse which lay beneath the veneer of "perfection." Problems remained hidden to outsiders. At other times the marriage lasted as long as it did because two disturbed people meshed so well together as long as they were sick. When one became "healthy" (e.g., the alcoholic who finally got help), the marriage fell apart at that point!

We have spoken of many elements for a happy conjugal life in the preceding sections. The presence of selfless love, communication, patience, and mutual responsibility are indigenous to what we label sacramental marriage. The absence, therefore, to a vital degree of any of these recognized essentials can only lead to marital failure. Indeed, one can foresee that a lack of one or other of the loving components needed for true marital bonding can raise legitimate questions about the very validity of the conjugal union itself. Just because one goes through a *wedding* ceremony it does not necessarily follow that a *marriage* has taken place. This cannot be stated too often or too emphatically: *A wedding is NOT a marriage!* Love requires more than a ceremony. Love requires a sharing of mind, heart, and will. To contract marriage one needs to do much more than simply fulfill the legal requirements. Those who wish to share life together must actually be willing to share themselves. Those who seek to marry ought to be willing, able, and eager not only to *want* to share life and love, but must *do* just that. The mere desire is not sufficient. The parties to marriage must be personally capable of delivering on the promises made at the wedding ceremony. "Love" is such a misused word that it has lost its meaning. When many say, "I love you," they are not referring to love. They are referring to whatever notion of "love" they possess at the time. Unfortunately, with growing regularity, what is said to be "love" today is not love at all.

Let us now turn our attention to examining the headings or grounds for annulment in the Roman Catholic Church. Those reading and reflecting upon these expanded grounds for annulment may discover, sadly, that they never really entered a valid marriage to begin with. Perhaps they are in a position now to prove this.

# Chapter Three

# FACTORS PERTAINING TO ANNULMENT

Those of us who studied the various headings of "marriage nullity" as we prepared for our comprehensive examinations in ecclesial law used a simple formula to remember the various topics. A marriage may be null because of:

Lack Of Canonical Form
The Presence Of An Impediment That Was Not Dispensed
Defect Of Consent To Marriage

*Defect of Consent* itself was divided into three sections: A person may have a *lack of knowledge* about marriage. There may be a *lack of will* (something affecting the person's choice to marry). Finally, there may be a *lack of capacity* in that the person is deemed incapable of marrying because of some serious emotional or mental disturbance.

Now each of the above sub-headings is also divided into three. Under *Lack of knowledge*, there is the ground of *ignorance* (when a person did not know that marriage is a permanent union between a man and a woman which is ordered to the procreation of children by means of some kind of sexual cooperation — canon 1096). Second, there is the ground of *error*, which means simply that a person married the wrong spouse. However, it also includes the notion, still being studied by ecclesial jurisprudence, that there was an error regarding an attribute or quality of the person whom one married — a serious error because the quality was not only an important one, it was a quality "directly and principally intended" by the person who made the mistake. So the "quality" takes on more importance than the "person" whom one decides to marry (canon 1097). Third, there is the ground of *fraud*. In Church Law fraud is a very specific and limited ground which was a new addition to the Code of Canon Law promulgated in 1983. As the law is written, a marriage would be invalid if a person were deceived by fraud, but the fraud must have been perpetrated to obtain the partner's consent to marry. The fraud must also be about some quality in the other party which by its very nature "can seriously disturb the partnership of conjugal life." The jurisprudence regarding this ground is still developing. Many questions are raised: Does this ground apply to persons married before the 1983 Code of Canon Law? What are those qualities that "can seriously disturb the partnership of conjugal life"? Would the existence of a sexual disease which one party decided to hide from the other until after the marriage ceremony be considered fraud? What about a woman who has had a child out of wedlock when she was a teenager and only reveals this to her new husband after they return from the honeymoon? Much work on this ground still needs to be done (canon 1098).

Under the heading of *lack of will* there are three categories. First of all there is the ground of *conditional consent*. If a person married but had some sort of mental reservation or condition attached to their consent, and this condition concerned something in the future which is opposed to the substance of the marriage, then the marriage would be invalid. As an example, although this would be extremely difficult to prove, suppose a woman married but only on condition that she would never have any children because she could not stand the thought of losing her figure or the pain of childbirth. Or suppose she made it clear that she would marry provided that were she ever to get pregnant, there had to be an abortion. These would be examples of conditional consent (canon 1102).

The second category is the ground of *simulation*. If a person at the time of the wedding, even though they are exchanging their vows and promising that theirs will be a faithful, exclusive, permanent and, God-willing, fruitful union, he or she is truly and positively intending just the opposite: I have no intention of being faithful, or I have no intention of ever being open to bringing new life into our marriage, or I have no intention that this be a permanent union. Then that marriage is invalid (canon 1101). Of course, proving what a person was actually intending when they were giving their consent to marriage can be a very difficult, if not impossible, task. One can understand why so many annulment petitions presented on this ground are turned down. Even if a person were later to admit to this, the Church is placed in a "Catch 22" situation: a person is now asking the Church to believe that at the time of the ceremony, when vows were exchanged, he or she was lying but now they are telling the truth.

The final category in this section is that of *force and fear* (canon 1103). If a person married either because they were forced, or if the marriage took place because of great fear of such force (even if such a threat might not have the same effect on anybody else) and, most importantly, if that person feels that he or she has *no choice* but is compelled to choose marriage to escape from the force being imposed or the fear that was being experienced, then the marriage is invalid. Once again, this is a very specific and limited ground for nullity and not as easily proved as one might think. The circumstance of a girl who finds herself pregnant and having to deal with this situation normally comes to mind when speaking of force or fear in the context of marriage. This will be discussed further on.

The last set of grounds under the heading of *Defect of Consent Due to a Lack of Capacity* is probably the most used in tribunals in North America. Again there are three categories. The first: that a marriage is invalid because one of the parties suffered from a *lack of sufficient reason*. Here one of the parties must be shown to have been suffering from a mental disturbance of such severity that he or she was not capable of positing a "human act."

The second part of this heading is perhaps the most used ground for nullity, namely, that a person suffered from a "grave *lack of discretion of judgment*" about the essential rights and obligations of marriage. When people speak of a marriage being declared null because of "immaturity," this is the ground that is being used even if they are not aware of it. We shall examine this in greater detail later. It is enough to point out that this seems to be the one that affects most of those who come to the tribunal to have their marriage examined. A couple of points ought to be mentioned at this juncture. This does not mean that a person is suffering from any specific psychological problem. Nor does it necessarily mean that the individual is lacking in discretion of judgment about other things. It refers specifically to a person's lack of discretion of judgment about the special and lifelong obligations of marriage. Finally it does not simply mean "I made a mistake in marrying her," or "If I knew then what I know now, I wouldn't have married him."

The last heading involves a marriage being declared null because one of the parties was "not capable of assuming the essential obligations of marriage due to causes of a psychic nature." This ground is sometimes referred to as lack of due capacity. At other times stress is put on the fact that the person is suffering from a serious psychological anomaly, and that this affects the person's ability to assume and thus fulfill the obligations of marriage.

What I have listed above is a summary, and a brief one at that, of various grounds for nullity. To explore all of them in detail would not only be tedious but would also defeat the purpose of this work which is to enable you, the reader, to reflect on your own marriage to see if there are possible reasons why you should be bringing a case to your diocesan tribunal.

## 1. LACK OF CANONICAL FORM

A few years ago, I would never have bothered to mention this as a possible ground for nullity because the law of the Church was so well known to Catholics and even non-Catholics. It is just assumed that Catholics must be married in the home parish of one of the two parties (usually the woman), and the exchange of vows must take place before a priest and two witnesses. The priest *receives* or witnesses those vows in the name of the Church. In our theology of marriage the priest does not "marry" the couple. The man and woman marry one another by the exchange of their wedding vows (or in more technical canonical language, their "exchange of consent" to marry).

Because marriage is a sacred institution, our Church takes sacred things seriously. That is why the ceremony of marriage (known as the "form" of marriage) and the keeping of records are detailed with rules. At times, I'm sure that these rules, to one who is not a member of the Church, appear excessive. A review of the history of the law or rule will usually reveal, however, that it was enacted in response to a problem that existed. It is the nature of any community to try to correct such problems especially where individuals might otherwise be harmed or have their rights violated. So there is a purpose to these regulations.

With that understanding, the law regarding the marriage ceremony, the usual "form" of marriage, is found in canon 1108. For a marriage to be valid, the ceremony must take place before one's parish priest (or of course the bishop of the diocese if he were involved) or a priest or deacon delegated by the parish priest or ordinary. Secondly the one and the same priest or deacon must ask for and receive (in the name of the Church) the expression or manifestation of the consent of the two parties.

Since 1971 it has been possible for a Catholic to receive permission to marry a person of another faith (or no religious tradition at all) in a non-Catholic ceremony. Technically this is called a "Dispensation from Canonical Form." If such permission were requested and granted for a particular wedding, then the parish priest need not be involved. As long as he prepares the couple as any couple who have made plans for a wedding, once that permission is given, then the couple may be married in the presence of the non-Catholic minister, rabbi, or even the civil official if this is what was requested. I raise this issue only to point out that when this permission is given, because the Church treats marriage as something sacred, usually strict limitations are placed. The ceremony must take place in the presence of a given minister, or it must be a public ceremony, etc. If the conditions that were strictly required were not met, then it is possible that the dispensation itself must be considered invalid, and that would render the marriage invalid. If this was the scenario of your marriage, I would bring up the question. Ask the person who is assisting you with your annulment petition to first of all check to see if the proper dispensation had been applied for. Second, were the conditions met as they were spelled out in the dispensation?

Another issue that has become disturbingly familiar to tribunal judges is the question of the officiating priest or deacon. As you have read, the parish priest or those priests and deacons assigned to a parish are considered to be the only ones who can assist at a marriage in their parish without any further permission. If another priest or deacon were to perform the ceremony, then that person needs the delegation of either the parish priest or the bishop of the diocese. This becomes necessary when a friend of the family, a relative of one of the parties, a former teacher or classmate, etc. is asked to perform the ceremony. We priests know that we need *delegation* from the pastor to officiate at the wedding. This requirement even applies to a priest who had been assigned to that parish but is now transferred and assigned to another ministry. The marriage register of the parish should show that such delegation was granted. If it were not granted, the marriage would be invalid. Just because the records do not indicate in writing that delegation was not granted does not automatically mean that, in fact, it was not. Someone would have to follow up on this point, speak with the parish priest or the officiating priest if this is still possible, or if they still recall the details. This type of thing should never happen, but as I indicated above unfortunately what should never occur, in fact, oftentimes does!

The marriage ceremony itself is a beautiful ritual. It really does not need improvement. As one gets older, one learns that making something "relevant" or "meaningful" can be a dictatorial attempt to impose one's own subjective standards on others. Many of the marriage ceremonies occurring in the 1960's and 1970's were quite "meaningful," but they may have been invalid.

Right before the couple exchange their consent, they are questioned by the officiating priest about their freedom of choice, their commitment to fidelity, and their openness to the possibility of children. Then their vows are exchanged. Please read these words carefully, and see the promises that lie behind them:

> Have you come here freely and without reservation to give yourselves to each other in marriage?
>
> Will you love and honor each other as man and wife for the rest of your lives?
>
> Will you accept children lovingly from God, and bring them up according to the law of Christ and His Church?
>
> (Vows)
> I_____, take you_____,
> to be my husband/wife. I promise to be true to you in good times and in bad, in sickness in health. I will love you and honor you all the days of my life.

In order to make the ritual more "personal" or "meaningful," there have been priests who have allowed couples to write their own wedding vows. Often the three preceding questions are eliminated or worded in such a way as to render them without their original meaning. I have studied a marriage vow where the couple promised one another that they would grow in the depth of their "personhood," never interfere in each other's career, render them sexual pleasure without fail, never make unreasonable demands on their time, and "to live with you in happiness and peace as long as our love shall last!"

This isn't merely a matter of editing a text for a ceremony. In my view, they do not address the *essential* properties of marriage: unity (fidelity) and indissolubility. Such wording perverts the meaning of the marriage covenant where a couple establish a partnership of their whole lives. This is a partnership which is ordered to both the good of the spouses and to the procreation and education of the children. I am making reference to canons 1055 and 1056 of the Code of Canon Law. More importantly, the point I am making is that those reworded "relevant" vows do not apply to "marriage" as the Church understands marriage. The couple is not giving consent to marriage. If your marriage vows were not taken from the marriage rite but were somehow created by yourself, your spouse, the priest, etc., then perhaps the marriage is invalid. Do you still have a copy of the vows? Can the witnesses to the ceremony recall them? Perhaps the ceremony was video-taped.

Another problem that I have seen on occasion occurs when there is a ceremony between a Catholic and a member of another faith. Often the minister or rabbi is invited to participate. Of itself this can be a wonderful sign of the compromise and added work that will be necessary when two people who are serious about their different religious commitments marry. The problem occurs during the exchange of consent. The law of the Church is very clear: whoever receives the vows in the name of the Church (whether it is the priest in his own church, or whether it is the visiting clergy person) *must* receive the vows of *both* parties. One cannot have the Catholic priest receive the vow of the Catholic party, and the non-Catholic receive the vow of the member of his or her church. It is not enough for this to have occurred with the priest still at the altar within hearing distance. The law is very strict on this point: the same person must receive the consent of both parties. If such switching occurred at your wedding (and this is easily proved now with the video taping of so many wedding ceremonies), then questions about the validity of your marriage must be raised on the basis that the proper canonical "form" was lacking.

I am sure that the reader may feel that some of these are strange scenarios. But I must assure you that they have occurred in the past. One might look on these as "loopholes" which some clever lawyer has devised. I won't argue that point, for it is more complex than it might appear to be. Let me just conclude by indicating that the various problematic wedding ceremonies that I have brought up should *never* be a problem. Any ordained person knows enough to receive delegation before he officiates at a marriage away from his own parish church. Nor is there a priest alive who is not aware that one cannot allow a "split" ceremony when an inter-faith marriage ceremony is taking place. Yet sometimes these events happen without warning or thought. Some priest or deacon who was supposed to arrive is delayed or forgets to come. Sometimes things happen in the midst of the most well-coordinated liturgy that catches everyone off guard.

This section was not included to accuse or demean anyone. I am not making sport of brother priests who have found themselves in a compromising situation and who, unfortunately, take a "chance" that no one will notice that some irregularity is taking place. I do think that Catholics have a right to know that, as a community of faith, we take marriage seriously. A wedding ceremony is not merely the precursor to a piece of paper called a marriage license. Marriage is a sacred society. Liturgy is the worship of God. Sacraments are sacred actions. All of these factors come into play when a wedding ceremony is taking place. Most ecclesial law that prescribes who can or cannot perform given actions is usually the result of some problem or abuse that took place in the past. We tend to make laws to correct past problems or to prevent them from happening again. If by chance something happened on the day of the wedding which should never have occurred, and if that has affected the very validity of the marriage, a person has a right to know this. That person also has a right to make use of this knowledge if it may help him or her to be reconciled once again to Christ and His Church.

## 2. THE IMPEDIMENTS TO MARRIAGE

There are certain conditions which render a person *incapable* of marriage. In canonical language these are called impediments. There is no need to go into depth on this issue. Most of the impediments established by Church, as opposed to natural, law are able to be dispensed. Some of them actually take into consideration situations that were more possible in another era and another culture. In our rather "sophisticated" modern culture, many of these impediments are hardly likely to ever have been an issue at all. For example, in Church Law there is a minimum age under which a man or woman may not marry. A man must have completed his sixteenth year or a woman must have completed her fourteenth year in order to marry validly. So a wedding ceremony between a fifteen year old boy and his twenty-one year old fiancee would be considered invalid unless there had been a dispensation granted. Common sense (hopefully) would demand that this situation never arise. Even were it to do so, I doubt there is a bishop who would ever grant such a dispensation or a priest who would officiate at such a wedding.

Some of the impediments have to do with blood relationship within which a marriage may not occur. Again common sense dictates the outcome. A brother-sister "marriage" is forbidden and is never dispensed. In the past second cousins needed a dispensation to marry, but since the 1983 Code of Church Law, this is no longer the case. Also prior to 1983 a person was forbidden to marry his or her godparent without a dispensation. This was called a "spiritual relationship" and required a dispensation. While this might seem to be an improbable event to happen in the first place, consider the Catholic woman who has been dating a Hindu gentleman. Because of her faith and commitment to the Lord, he is so impressed that he takes instructions and becomes a baptized Roman Catholic. If he had chosen his fiancee as his sponsor, that would have created the impediment. There are other situations that sometimes arise which are usually dispensed, e.g. a Catholic marrying a non-baptized person requires a dispensation. A Catholic marrying a non-Catholic Christian also requires permission to do so. In both events, these are usually granted.

There is, however, an impediment that can indeed exist which was unknown by one or both parties. It can also happen that one party was aware of it and the other was purposely not informed. I am referring to the impediment of *impotence* which is not only an impediment of Church Law, but is considered one of natural law as well. This means that this is an impediment that cannot be dispensed.

IMPOTENCY

It is not altogether uncommon that sexual difficulties constitute a grave threat to the viable future of a marital union. It matters little whether the sexual difficulty originates with a physical defect or is traceable to psychological causes. What is important is that in marriage the sexual dimension constitutes an intrinsic component of conjugal life and, since it is the most profound means of sharing love, any obstruction or deviation in this delicate area redounds to the very core of the marital union. For this reason, sexual problems are closely allied with invalidity. The *crucial* factor in an annulment proceeding is that the alleged sexual difficulty has proven to be a major block to the establishment of a loving and mutual relationship, and that this difficulty has been present (even potentially) through the marriage from the beginning.

Let us begin at the outset to clarify a frequently mistaken notion. *Impotence is not sterility.* Sterility does not constitute impotence. Many believe that the inability to procreate due to the physical absence or debility of sperm or ova constitutes impotency.

This is simply not true. The inability to procreate is what is labeled *sterility*. At times sterility and impotency will coexist in a person so that one is rendered incapable of both adequately performing the sexual act and also incapable of procreating due to a defect in sperm or ova. However, *only impotency* of itself invalidates marriage. Sterility, under normal circumstances, does not. (One possible occasion when sterility is foreseen in law as a cause of nullity will be discussed below.)

Impotency is a very complex medical and/or psychological defect. It does not lend itself to facile discussion or resolution. Since impotence is a medical and/or psychological matter, the fact of its presence is best left to the judgment of the competent authorities. What we are concerned with here is the fact of impotency as a ground for Church annulment.

### (a) Impotency in the Male

The inability of a man to have or sustain an erection of the penis and to ejaculate into a woman's vagina is the operative definition of male impotency. What is at issue is the ability to perform the sexual act. Impotency is commonly held to be divided into two classes: (1) *organic*, and (2) *functional*. Organic impotence is present when the actual sexual organ itself is deformed or in some way organically defective. In functional impotency, even though the sexual organs remain physically and organically intact, for some reason they do not function in a normal manner.

Examples of organic impotency would be:

1. Lack of a penis.
2. Irregular formation of the penis so that it cannot be inserted into the vagina, because:
   a) It is too large for the woman's vagina;
   b) The penis is so crooked (the so-called "bent nail syndrome") as to prevent its being inserted into the woman's vagina;
   c) There is no opening in the head of the penis.

3. Any defect in the penis, testicle, or the sperm ducts which would prevent some fluid from being ejaculated. There is no longer sperm impotency. (Here note that while this also constitutes sterility, it is not the only form of sterility. A very low sperm count can render one sterile insofar as he cannot impregnate a woman. But while an extremely low sperm count is sterility, it does not of itself constitute impotency.)

*Examples of functional impotency in the male:*

1. The dysfunction of sexual organ due to any form of lower body paralysis. An injury to the central nervous system which affects the sexual functioning of a man renders him impotent.
2. Sexual dysfunction due to a psychological cause.
   a) Premature ejaculation
   b) No ejaculation due to some emotional difficulty.
   c) Inability to have or sustain an erection long enough to perform the sexual act.

*How can one prove impotency?*

To prove your case you will generally need:

1. *Your own testimony* to the condition of impotence.
2. Hopefully, your impotent *partner's statement* of the condition. At times this can be difficult. Many persons are too embarrassed to admit they are, or were at the time of the marriage, impotent.
3. *Witnesses* who are relatives or friends with whom the impotent party spoke and to whom he related the presence of a sexual problem.
4. *Expert witnesses*, namely a doctor's report (if the husband was treated or spoke to a doctor). This could be either a medical doctor or a psychologist or psychiatrist. Or, the husband may be willing to submit to a medical

and/or psychological examination for the purpose of obtaining the annulment, which may also help him medically and/or psychologically.

If your husband has had this problem and your marriage has fallen apart consult your tribunal in your diocesan Chancery or Pastoral Care Office for assistance in the possible attaining of a Church annulment.

### (b) Impotency in the Female

Since impotency in the female is relatively the same in cause as impotency in the male, and since essentially the same proofs for annulment are required, we will limit our present discussion to the fact of female impotency and its form.

For the purpose of our study, female impotence is defined as the incapacity of a woman to have sexual intercourse. A woman must be capable of receiving the erect penis within her vagina. Therefore she must have a vagina (even an artificial one). As long as the vagina is capable of receiving the deposit of some fluid from the act of sexual intercourse, then the woman is potent. This condition does not have to have been manifested prior to marriage if a woman were not capable of knowing of the condition. As long as the condition was present that somehow prevents her from having sexual intercourse, then she is impotent. (For a more in-depth study, see Fr. Lawrence Wrenn's excellent, if somewhat technical but well-structured and readable, book on annulments which was first published in 1970 and is presently in its fifth revised edition: *Annulments*, Washington, D.C.: Canon Law Society of America, 1988, pp. 12-18.)

It is clearly evident that the inability to copulate renders a person impotent. Fertility is not the issue here. If the woman cannot for some physical or psychological reason consummate the marriage, then she is understood to be impotent. The forms of impotence in the female are more extensive than the categories of impotency affecting the male. Here are a few examples. If a woman were born *without* a true, properly functioning vagina, i.e., she lacked a vagina, she is impotent. If there were some *defect* in the size or shape of the vagina so that, by being too narrow, too small, etc., she is not capable of receiving the male organ, again this constitutes impotency. There are other examples, and again I would refer the reader to Father Wrenn's work, *Annulments.*

*Examples of functional impotency in the female:*

This refers mainly to *vaginismus*, the recurrent or persistent involuntary spasm of the musculature of the outer third of the vagina that interferes with coitus. It is a painful disorder which affects a woman's ability and desire to have sexual intercourse and makes the insertion of the penis difficult or impossible. It is a dysfunction which is not caused exclusively by a physical disorder but seems to result from psychological causes which produce these involuntary muscle spasms in the vagina whenever the male approaches the female to perform the sexual act. The causes for this psychological reaction are numerous and only after careful examination can one ascertain the reasons why the woman so reacts.

The requirements for proof of female impotency are substantially the same as those for the male. Again the tribunal should be given the facts for examination since they alone are in a position to render adequate judgment, taking into account all the various complexities of this type of case.

If your wife suffered from an organic or functional form of impotency, or if you are a woman who suffered from this condition, submit your case to the tribunal. There is a good chance that your marriage can be annulled. There is a principle that became a part of the jurisprudence of the Church back in 1949 which is often quoted in cases involving female impotency: "Just as no one is legally bound to undergo a surgical operation which would endanger one's life, so no one is legally bound to have intercourse which would necessarily involve intolerable pain" (*S.R.R.*, Dec., *c*. Heard, 12/30/49 in *Ephemerides Iuris Canonici*, VIII (1951) 3-4, p. 363).

## 3. MARRIAGES NULL BECAUSE OF A DEFECT OF CONSENT

In the introductory section of this chapter, I briefly touched on this complex area. The nine categories which are a part of ecclesial law were mentioned, although to be honest many of those situations foreseen in law have little application to modern life. It would be very difficult, for example, to imagine that any adult in our sexually saturated culture was not aware (lacked the minimal knowledge) that marriage is a union of a man and a woman that involves some kind of physical sexual intimacy.

The most important or at least the most used grounds alleging the nullity of a marriage involve the new canon in the Code of Church Law: canon 1095. It reads:

They are incapable of contracting marriage:

1. who lack the sufficient use of reason;
2. who suffer from grave lack of discretion of judgment concerning essential matrimonial rights and duties which are to be mutually given and accepted.
3. who are not capable of assuming the essential obligations of matrimony due to causes of a psychic nature.

A lot of ink has been and will continue to be spilled over both the interpretation and the significance of this law. Already analyses and commentaries abound. Sides have been drawn up indicting liberal, moderate, and conservative interpretations and applications of the law to marriage annulment cases.

Rather than burden the reader with all of the possible interpretations of this law, I will simply offer the thoughts of a respected canonist who in 1986 published an excellent commentary and reflection on the marriage canons of the Code of Canon Law. Fr. Ladislaus Orsy, S.J. is a respected professor, author, and jurist. In his *Marriage in Canon Law: Text and Comments, Reflections and Questions* (Collegeville, MN: Liturgical Press), he proposed a marvelous explanation that reflects not only the "theory" of law, but also would touch a responsive chord in all who have ever been married. His explanation brings a person to the moment of the wedding and to focus on how the reality of that moment was experienced:

> Briefly, the overall meaning of the canon is that a person intending to marry must have the capacity to think rationally, to decide responsibly, and to carry out the decision by action. This capacity must be present *at the moment of the exchange of the promises*. If the validity of the promises is ever doubted, all that has happened before and all that has followed later can only serve as signs to determine the precise spirit of the person at the moment of the exchange of the promises (p. 130).

Although any person can take part in a wedding ceremony, a person must have the capacity to marry for that marriage to be valid. Although having the proper intentions is also required, that is not enough. A priest I know makes the point which Catholics might better understand: We are familiar in our understanding of the sacraments that a person must have the ability as well as the right intention. If my grandmother, with all the right intentions and in all good faith, pronounced the words of the Eucharistic consecration ("This is my body") over bread at table for a week, the bread would still remain a loaf of bread. A person must have the capacity (in the example he uses, ordination to the priesthood) and not just the right intention for the sacrament to be valid.

Fr. Orsy explains that this *incapacity* that would disqualify a person from marriage is viewed from differing perspectives. The exact meaning of the canon is developing as our jurisprudence develops. The situations which affect a marriage that ends up in our tribunals will ultimately be the source of the reflection and development of our jurisprudence. The first point is that a person who lacks the use of reason is not capable of marriage. Secondly, a person who might have the use of reason but for circumstances which may be situational, developmental, or emotional, "they cannot form a judgment either about marriage in general or about this union in particular" (ibid., p. 131). The third category refers to those who lack the psychological capacity to take on the essential duties of marriage. Here marriage is not looked upon as some impossible ideal, nor is it viewed as a "soap opera" or any other "fad" type of union. Marriage is viewed as a partnership of life that is ordered to the good of the spouses as well as the procreation and education of any children that may be born from it.

This canon is the basis for many of the grounds of nullity that are used in our tribunals. Several examples of how the lived experience of troubled unions have led to an affirmative decision and a declaration of nullity by a Church court. I do want the reader to keep one important aspect in mind. Ours is a world which seems to have produced persons demanding instant gratification. There is a pervasive attitude, not only among the young, which views life in this fashion: I want what I want when I want it! There is also much misunderstanding about Church annulments. How could a marriage of over twenty years be declared null? How can a marriage with children be annulled? How come my case had grounds but my brother's case did not? Is any marriage at all possible fodder for some "annulment mill"? These are legitimate concerns. Pope John Paul in his 1987 address to the Roman Rota reminded that court: "For the canonists, the principle must remain clear that only *incapacity* and not *difficulty* in giving consent and realizing a true community of life and love invalidates a marriage" (cf. *The Pope Speaks*, vol. 2, 1987, p. 131). This principle of Church Law must be used properly. In my experience most priests who have the assignment (and burden) to make decisions on annulment cases when this canon is operative do so seriously. If it is humanly possible to prove this ground, and if it reflects the truth that this marriage was not just an unhappy one but was indeed invalid because one or both of the parties really did not have the ability to marry, then they will render an affirmative decision allowing an annulment.

This ground is manifested in many different circumstances. I will offer a number of them for your reflection. This is not meant, in any fashion, to be an exhaustive list. Nor does the mere mention of one of these circumstances "prove" nullity of itself without confirming testimony. I hope that, in these examples, it will become clear that because of the situation cited, a person was either lacking the discretion or maturity of judgment needed for marriage, or was unable to fulfill the obligations of marriage. If any of these examples refer to your own lived experience, then you ought to consult your diocesan tribunal.

## (A) INTOXICATION AT THE TIME OF THE WEDDING CEREMONY

There are, of course, many levels of intoxication due to a person's alcohol intake. The degree of drunkenness is determined by medical science on the percentage of alcohol within one's bloodstream. Since alcohol is generally absorbed into the blood at a rather fast pace, the number of drinks one ingests within a given time will determine the "quickness" of intoxication as well as the degree thereof.

Many factors enter into becoming intoxicated. These vary from the amount of alcohol ingested to the time frame within which the drinks were consumed to the amount of food within one's stomach. (Since this radically affects the absorption rate of alcohol into the bloodstream, the more food in the stomach the slower the absorption, the slower the rate of intoxication.) The type of alcohol consumed, the person's size and build, as well as their physical and emotional condition are all further factors still.

The blood will carry the ingested alcohol to the liver which burns up alcohol at a steady pace (somewhere around one ounce per hour). But when the level of alcohol exceeds this rate, the liver cannot but burn off an ounce at a time and the rest continues to flow in the bloodstream, eventually ending up in the brain. The result is intoxication in one of several degrees.

The discussion of alcohol intoxication as a grounds for possible annulment is a tricky area of jurisprudence, and therefore we have chosen to precede our legal observation with a short statement about the nature of alcohol reaction in different persons.

It happens, not infrequently, that one or other party to a marriage is intoxicated at the moment in the ceremony when consent is exchanged. Since in Canon Law, proper rational consent is absolutely crucial for the validity of a marriage, then it stands to reason that if one of the parties to a marriage was intoxicated at the ceremony, the marriage can be declared null and void by a Church court.

What type of intoxication are we speaking of here? What degree of drunkenness is required to invalidate a marriage? Strictly speaking, one must be "quite intoxicated." Just "feeling good" or "having a good buzz" is not usually sufficient. This "feeling good" perhaps is indicative of other things and, with sufficient examination, that may indicate invalidity due to another source. A pretty well defined intoxication might be characterized by blurred vision, poor motor reflex (perhaps the person needs assistance in walking up the aisle), etc. This stage of intoxication might be indicated by unusual behavioral patterns, or a change in personality to some degree. If any of these factors were present at the time of your wedding, then I suggest that the tribunal be given a chance to examine your marriage for possible invalidity.

Furthermore the reason and motivation for a person's getting drunk comes into play in the judgment of invalidity. Perhaps the marriage partner was a frequent heavy drinker. If this were the case, perhaps the spouse was an alcoholic. This might indicate one approach to the case — when the disease of alcoholism is present. Perhaps the party to your marriage got drunk in order to "get it over with," or perhaps even to do what he or she really didn't intend — get married. The *why* he or she became intoxicated on the wedding day at the time of the ceremony may indicate a deeper problem, and it is the deeper problem which may indeed interfere with a person's being able to give consent to marriage. Without that ability to give consent, there would be no marriage.

Moreover, it should be noted that today, especially, intoxication at the ceremony might be due to an excessive intake of narcotics, pills, legal or illegal drugs with various degrees of potency. Alcohol is not the only form of intoxication. Drugs are yet another. The same rules apply to intoxication from drugs that apply to alcohol. Again, the "why" of taking drugs as well as the amount and type could be a critical factor in the determination of marital invalidity.

How do you go about proving that there existed intoxication at the time of the wedding ceremony? First, the best way is to call upon some relatives or friends who might be willing to testify to the fact before a Church court. This would be done either in person, by deposition, or in whatever way the priest who is judge in the case determines. Secondly, it always helps to have the allegedly intoxicated party to admit to his/her being in such a state during the ceremony. However, this is not essential to the outcome of a case. Another possibility of proof, would be to present a video tape of the ceremony in which signs (if not outright proof) of intoxication on the part of one of the parties at the altar are apparent.

If your broken marriage took place under these circumstances, you should submit your case to your local tribunal and have them review its merits. Perhaps an annulment can be obtained on this basis. Perhaps upon investigation, yet further grounds for annulment will likewise be uncovered. It is clearly to one's advantage to have the Church's legal experts examine your marriage in light of the incident that occurred at the ceremony itself. I also would repeat at this time that what has been stated about alcohol intoxication at the time of the ceremony would also apply to a person who is under the influence of drugs such as cocaine, marijuana and even prescription medicines, depending upon their effect on one's mind and behavior.

## (B) ALCOHOLISM

There has been much discussion of late concerning alcoholism and its effects. Medical science has conducted extensive testing in the area of alcohol and its effects upon bodily function, especially its slow destruction of brain cells. The social sciences have likewise engaged in the intensive study of alcoholism as it affects the social fiber of this country and the world, especially the family unit. Sociologists now conclude that alcoholism not only destroys the individual so affected, but also his or her entire family as a unity and can have lasting effects upon individual members of the family, especially young children. There is much literature today reflecting upon the experiences and shared character traits that so many children coming from an alcoholic background (a person often referred to as an A.C.O.A. — an Adult Child of an Alcoholic) seem to share. Psychology enters the picture by analyzing the effects of alcohol upon individual behavior patterns as well as the negative psychological effects that behavior has upon other members of society who intimately interact with the alcoholic. Alcoholism has been classified as a *disease* by most professionals in the medical and behavioral sciences. The conclusion therefore is that alcoholism is more than mere rampant intemperance. It is an uncontrollable impulse to engage in a form of self-destruction, though perhaps the alcoholic is not consciously aware of trying to destroy himself. The bottom line is that he does, however, usually manage not only to destroy himself but his home and family as well.

Since alcoholism is a disease, and since it is compulsive behavior which appears to be present constitutionally in some people, then it therefore seems to constitute a radical impairment to the exchanging of matrimonial consent. Also, the alcoholic, because he has no control over his "problem" will in some cases have an incapacity to assume or fulfill the obligations promised in the marriage ceremony. So while *alcoholism* of itself may not be the specific ground of nullity, the presence, severity, and effects of the disease as it affects a person's ability to give consent to marriage or to live out its essential obligations becomes the basis of the annulment: either that a person lacked the discretion of judgment necessary regarding the essential matrimonial rights and duties or the person was incapable of assuming the obligations of marriage.

It is important to note that not everyone who drinks is an alcoholic. Not everyone who drinks or who is an alcoholic is incapable of marriage. Social drinkers, heavy drinkers, excessive drinkers, or even all alcoholics cannot be "written off" wholesale as incapable of marriage. As the jurisprudence has been developing, it has taken great pains to distinguish among the various stages of alcoholism, making a clear distinction between alcohol abuse and alcohol dependence. Health care professionals have to use this distinction in their treatment of the alcoholic.

In its most serious form, chronic or irreversible alcoholism as the sole "ground" of nullity requires that there be available evidence as to the presence of the most severe stages of the disease. I would also add that heavy or excessive drinking in any form may indicate a seriously irresponsible personality. Grounds might be present for a Church annulment based, not on alcohol dependence but due to some psychological irregularity. Whenever marital problems have arisen in the context of drinking, a tribunal review of one's marriage is clearly in order.

I present this as an example of how ecclesiastical jurisprudence has approached this issue in the past. It is a decision of the Roman Rota written by Sabattoni and dated February 24, 1961 which is required reading for all who study Canon Law today. It posits as classic certain signs and characteristics of chronic alcoholism. Perhaps it will help you judge the presence or absence of alcoholism in your marriage as it may relate to grounds for an annulment:

> Chronic alcoholism is characterized by a complete decline of the intellect, of the memory and will, as a result of which the victim appears indifferent, unstable, incapable of concentrating attention or of persevering in a

job; and by the loss of the ethical sense causing a deviation of personality. The alcoholic gradually loses his self-respect, becomes careless about his person and about the approval of others, cynical, disaffectionate, cruel and obscene.

Sexual weakness resulting from the abuse of alcohol not infrequently leads an individual to acts of perversion by which he attempts to satisfy his persistent libido. Under this complexity of psychic degeneration definite syndromes emerge among which are delirious forms of a persecution complex, especially quarrels or showdowns with his wife (or husband), rages of jealousy.... These may be considered the observable characteristics or effects.

How does one judge the degree of seriousness attending to alcoholism? What barometer is applied to compute the data whereby chronic alcoholism can be determined or proven in court?

(1) First, the Church court will look for signs of behavioral irregularities and physical impairment. Some symptoms of chronic alcoholism would be occasional blackouts, problems in walking, motor control, the feelings of "pins and needles" in the extremities, involuntary tremors of the face, hands, mouth, trouble speaking, etc.

(2) Second, the Church court will try to determine how long the disease has been present with the person. Of course, there is no surefire yardstick to determine the exact duration of this illness, since the degree of symptoms of alcoholism vary in time with individual nature and physical makeup. However, once the signs of chronic alcoholism are visible we presume that the problem has been a long-standing one.

(3) Third, medical records are always helpful to a tribunal's review of a case. These records supplement the verbal

testimony of the parties and their witnesses and serve as
expert testimony to present further proof regarding a
case for nullity. So look for the number of times a person
has been hospitalized for either physical or mental
reasons.

*How does one go about proving the case?*

— Testimony of the parties (husband and/or wife)
— Confession of alcoholism from the one suffering its
effects. Since any person suffering from alcoholism
almost never admits his problem, if the alcoholic con-
fesses his problem, a Church court would view this with
a presumption that the confession is true.
— Testimony of witnesses. They might be able to describe
what behavioral characteristics they themselves wit-
nessed when in the presence of the alcoholic party.
Testimony reflecting any experiences prior to your
marriage would of course be most helpful. The total
picture is important. What occurred before you married
is even more crucial than the problems present during
the union.
— Medical records: If the alcoholic spouse has been
hospitalized for drinking or its effects, perhaps the
medical records could be released to the tribunal. This is
not always easily obtained.
— Police records: Frequently, the alcoholic gets in trouble
with the authorities over his drinking. The violation of
law can cover the gambit from drunk and disorderly
conduct, to motor vehicle offenses, to acts of sexual
deviation. The presence of a police record based on
offenses relating to alcohol can be a great help in leading
to a legal presumption that chronic alcoholism was
indeed present in your marriage.

A marriage can be proven null and void when the above criteria is in evidence or one or the other of the above mentioned areas can be substantiated beyond a reasonable doubt. Experience has clearly demonstrated that if one is an alcoholic, it can be proven in a Church court. Again, the reminder that because one is a heavy drinker does not mean that the person is an alcoholic. However, the drinking may indicate a psychological irregularity which should be examined by a Church court.

Please always keep in mind, too, that in order to prove that a marriage is null and void, it must be evident that this was so from the time the marriage took place. If alcoholism or heavy drinking was present from the very beginning of your marriage and was responsible to a vital degree in your marital failure, consult the tribunal of your diocese. You may have a case.

## A Pastoral Essay: The Alcoholic Parent — It's the Children Who Suffer

One has only to look to court records, treatment centers, rehabilitation programs, delinquency centers, etc. to find readily available the prolific evidence that an alcoholic family produces damaging effects on the offspring. Counselors in almost any field of pastoral psychology can attest first hand to the influence an alcoholic parent can exert upon an individual child's personality development. While the family situation spoken of will not produce an alcoholic child unless the child himself has an addictive tendency already existing within his genetic makeup and personality, still the fact that this child can and often does become delinquent, in any and all areas, from school to morals, can be denied only at the expense of proving oneself at the very best naive.

The family is radically affected by the presence of alcoholism. Spiritually, physically, emotionally, socially and economically, the family suffers tremendously. The most disturbing and effective characteristic of this type of situation is that the warm love and tenderness so necessary for normal growth and development are painfully absent. Trust in himself and certainly in his self-confidence receive death blows; the child has no one but himself to rely upon for that much needed direction, care and affection. Oftentimes the child will seek the help necessary (this drive for love and growth is inherent in the human personality and is so imperative that the person always seeks this in some way) for personality perfection outside the context of his or her own family life and — as can be attested by doctors, clergy, and counselors — seldom accomplishes adequately (even with assistance) what is possible in the truly normal family structure. The search frequently leads one to "hang out" with the wrong crowd and learn from them all the wrong answers.

Just how debilitating this situation will be depends on a battery of variables: the person's psychological makeup, temperament, former education and influence, physical constitution, financial situation within the home, the relation and effect of other siblings and so forth. Although alcoholism, per se, is not inherited, the above factors coupled with how the problem was, or is, being handled by the parent in question will determine the child's degree of social, psychological, and spiritual adaptability.

Is there a predisposition for alcoholism? Probably, and there is some indication of this in recent studies in genetics. Also it seems that the alcoholic atmosphere of the home, about which we have been speaking, may encourage a child's alcoholic tendencies if he or she remains within that situation. But whether it determines or causes his or her future relationship to drink is dubious.

The natural psychological development of the child lends credence to the belief that environment works with genetics to shape the individual and produces in this case undesirable effects. The total trust and confidence placed in the parent by the child at an early stage of growth is a key to healthy behavior. When, however, this confidence and trust is lost through the action of one or both parents, then the child experiences a feeling of guilt and fear: loss of self-esteem accompanies these feelings and consequently the child becomes threatened from within as well as from without, subsequently producing insecurity which seems to be a symptom, if not a definite cause, of alcoholic behavior and personality.

Moral behavior is directly proportional to the values of the parents which are appropriated to oneself during the formative years. Children, as they grow, ultimately choose for themselves what kind of lifestyle they will follow and toward what type of goal their life thrust will be orientated. They internalize to a great extent the mores of the culture communicated to them through the family situation and parental influences. The standards of right and wrong, good and evil which parents call their own inevitably become at least essentially the child's. The point here is that, within the confines of an alcoholic family, many and various attitudes of mind and codes of behavior become impressed upon the children as they incorporate their own life experiences with that of those around them or with whom they identify. The alcoholic personality creates an unreal situation in regard to the possibility of normal growth patterns and, consequently, inhibits the children from ever experiencing the gentle, tender, and warm love so necessary for true growth and the proper attitude toward good and evil that will allow them to see clearly what is right and to be done or wrong and to be avoided. The inherent law of human nature that the human person always seeks the good, that the basic tendency is to do good and to avoid evil, can never be adequately grasped by the individual child who has always experienced a dubious morality. It is not that the child is determined or fated for spiritual or psychic doom, but the child's vision of conduct is at best clouded, because the fundamental education and most influential teacher has failed to be a father or mother in the manner proper to true parental love, to the necessary parental obligations.

Frequently, as children near adolescence and want to be with, and part of, people other than their own immediate family, they find the process of integrating into the social-psychological context of peer groups beyond their ability to control and adequately handle. This process becomes extremely difficult. It's difficult enough for the child of an "ideal" family situation and a "normal" home life, but for the children of alcoholic parents — because of a basic insecurity and fear ingrained in their lives throughout the formative years — it is even more troublesome. A certain amount of hate for the parent responsible for this problem emerges to create a basic hostility toward the family which is often taken out on friends. The carryover of maladjustment from one area to another is made very easy by the situation itself. This often results in confused roles which possibly can find their origin in the "status" which the child desires for himself or herself because it has neither been acquired per se (in the normal sociological sense of the term) nor achieved (accomplished by personal effort).

Family members play their roles as they understand them but, because of the alcoholic member, the roles become aberrations and give the wrong impressions. The different roles of family members should be mutually supportive and well-defined. But, because of the drunk, they lack these directive and supportive elements and become, at best, loosely defined. All this creates a rigid and unsupportive personality. The tension, sorrow, and conflict so characteristic of an alcoholic home stifles growth and effects a sense of incompleteness and inferiority which could haunt the members for the rest of their days. Children in such an environment tend to become uncreative and unimaginative and to fall into a psychological and sociological rut.

The children of an alcoholic parent can be helped and guided by trained professionals, yet it takes a great deal more than mere expertise and interest to rehabilitate the child of alcoholism. The basic point of reference always remains the family unit. In order to properly assist and adequately overcome the problem situation, it becomes necessary to cure the family as a whole. For unless the tension and conflict, worry and anger, hatred and insecurity that so typify such a family are rectified and eliminated, the hope for a viable and productive therapy is virtually nil. The parents themselves must be helped by the professional, and assuming that help is sought and cooperation is positive, the family unit itself can benefit and the individual person involved assisted in life readjustment.

It would seem that the separation of the child from such a poor atmosphere is a prerequisite for any attempt at therapy. Once done, then the parents themselves can be treated while at the same time giving the children the break necessary for proper disposition to therapy. A child away from alcoholism is a child that cannot be influenced by it. The move is, of course, temporary but absolutely necessary if the process of growth is to be achieved and ever to have any promise of success.

The unfortunate aspect of alcoholism is that the alcoholic usually will never admit to this problem, much less to seek treatment for it, until he "hits bottom." Once he experiences his state as devoid of joy and promise then and only then will the average alcoholic seek help. Until such time, it is the children who suffer most severely from lack of love and the desire to be what they have been destined to become: normal, healthy children of God.

By way of conclusion, let me add my experience in the pastoral judicial ministry in the tribunal. It never ceases to amaze me how the patterns are repeated time and time again. I cannot begin to relate how many cases have been presented before me that involved a person who was the child of one or both alcoholic parents. I have seen how other siblings seem to have the same distorted approach to life that the person whom I am attempting to assist has. How many children of alcoholics go on to flee a destructive, abusive, dangerous home environment only to marry a person with the same tendencies toward alcohol abuse. The person repeats the tragedy that was experienced at home. Children are born to this union, and now the pattern goes on for another generation. As if this were not bad enough, I have also experienced the scenario whereby the person now flees her alcoholic marriage (as she had fled the abusive home environment) and goes on to a second marriage: to another alcoholic. And on it goes! Damaged persons find or create damaged relationships.

(c) EPILEPSY

Certainly epilepsy is one of the least understood illnesses. For decades people who suffered from epileptic seizures were characterized as insane and frequently treated like animals. Fortunately advances in the medical and psychological sciences have shed light upon epilepsy as a disorder of the brain and nervous system. Nonetheless, this disorder remains highly complex and profoundly difficult to explain to any lay person's satisfaction. Clearly, it takes a doctor to understand all the many complexities of epilepsy, so we shall discuss this topic only briefly, highlighting the main points voiced in annulment cases, based upon this disorder.

Epilepsy is characterized essentially by convulsive attacks originating in the central nervous system of the higher brain stem. In his 5th revised edition of *Annulments*, Fr. Wrenn gives this definition: "Epilepsy may be defined as a disordered regulation of energy release within the brain entailing the periodic appearance of a recurring pattern of short-lived disturbances of consciousness, typically accompanied by unrestrained motor activity" (p. 30).

Although there are various forms and stages of the disorder, a central element remains throughout which has particular import for tribunal personnel. The element of which I speak is the effect of epilepsy which dulls, vitiates, or otherwise impairs the mind and which may prevent a person from giving proper consent to a marriage.

In the extreme, epilepsy is a major brain disorder which leaves the afflicted with a psychotic mental state tantamount to insanity. However, the important factor for our discussion is that while an epileptic seizure usually lasts for a short interval, it can leave temporary effects which impair a person's mental and motor process for days.

Therefore, if a person who suffers from epilepsy undergoes a seizure immediately prior to their wedding ceremony (this could be from a few days before to the wedding day itself), their brain could be so impacted as to prevent their exchanging proper matrimonial consent. Remember, if consent is not properly exchanged, the marriage is null and void because the act of giving consent was itself defective.

If by chance in your marriage you or your partner suffer from epilepsy and sustained a seizure just prior to the wedding ceremony, you may have a chance for obtaining a Church annulment.

As an aside: there are situations of epilepsy in which a person is rendered mentally ill by the disorder. This, too, would render a marriage null and void. These types of cases, however, would require much more detailed explanations, so we omit them here. It is enough that the concept of epilepsy as a ground for annulment (because it may have been the cause of a defect of consent) has been posited and the reader made aware of the possibility for a resolution of his or her marriage difficulty in a Church court on this ground.

Once the tribunal has been approached and your case introduced, the priest will then discuss with you what will be needed to prove your case on this basis.

### (D) THE "PSYCHIC" OR "PSYCHOLOGICAL" BASIS FOR ANNULMENT (CANON 1095)

With the advent of psychology in the last century, but particularly in view of the tremendous advance in this science over the past few decades, we have come to understand to a profound degree, the intrinsic effects a mental or emotional disorder has upon one's entering and sustaining a valid marriage. The Church, which has long accepted the valid conclusions of medical science, has not dragged its feet in admitting psychological disorders as a basis for Church annulments. In fact, the frequency of annulments based upon psychiatric causes has grown so steadily in the past several years, that one could be astounded at the high percentage of marriages which break up due to a psychological impairment. One wonders if perhaps many marriages are being entered into which, unfortunately, have no business taking place at all. Even so, what comes across clearly to those involved in marriage work is that many, many marriages today that go "on the rocks" can trace their failure to some form of psychological cause.

Many forms of psychological irregularities exist, all of which can ultimately lead to marital breakdown sooner or later. What characterizes these irregularities is a profound lack of maturity, discretion, freedom, rational thinking, etc. The psychological disorder does not have to be so grave as to constitute what classically might have been referred to as insanity. All that need be present is a disorder serious enough to render one either lacking the full capacity to posit proper and true matrimonial consent at the time of the wedding ceremony, or the inability to fulfill the obligations of marriage promised in the wedding ceremony. This state of psychological impairment does not have to be so extreme as to always be on the level of a psychosis. On the other hand, this is not merely on the level of some personality quirks or flaws to which we are all prone. While a man might be a slob or a lousy cook, and while a woman might snore loudly or play on too many softball teams in the summer, these habits, irritating as they are, do not render a person psychologically incapable of marriage.

It is one thing to say, "I want to marry you," but it is quite another to be able to sustain an ordered married life with all the responsibility this entails. What poses for love before the wedding may not be love at all when it is asked to stand the test of time or the pressure of responsible conjugal living. What we are saying is that simply knowing what marriage is supposed to be and actually being able to live it with a single, chosen partner can be two entirely distinct situations. One might be in a sufficient mental state to desire a particular job but unable to perform the desired work when it comes down to it. Usually the person gets fired or quits. This is the way it can be for some people when choosing marriage: they want to marry but once wedded, find themselves unable to live up to the demands of married life. On occasion I have read a comment in the depositions that a given petitioner in a marriage case writes, and it is so sad because it illustrates the simple truth that "feeling" is very often mistaken for "reality." "Of course I was ready for marriage; after all, I was in love!"

Any form of serious mental illness may lead, upon investigation, to grounds for a Church annulment. While not every person afflicted with a mental or emotional disorder is an appropriate subject for an annulment, nevertheless, today the greater majority of cases introduced into a Church court find a favorable resolution after the tribunal judge thoroughly examines the merits of a particular case. Given valid psychological grounds for annulment, the overwhelming percentage of persons provide the necessary facts to prove their case in a tribunal. Therefore if your broken marriage was plagued by attitude, actions, and circumstances which would lead you to believe that some serious form of psychological impairment was present in your conjugal union, then it would serve you well to bring your case before the diocesan tribunal. The tribunal will then examine the merits of your case.

It is well beyond the scope of a book of this nature to attempt to classify all the various types of emotional or mental disorders that could, should, or would impact upon a person's ability to either give consent to marriage or fulfill the obligations of married life. The latest edition of the *Diagnostic and Statistical Manual of Mental Disorders* (referred to as the D.S.M. III - R) describes and attempts to provide in an orderly fashion (which I am sure can be helpful to the professional in the field) the various categories according to age, etiology, etc. A brief glance provides descriptions of organic disorders, psychoactive substance use disorders, schizophrenia, other psychotic disorders, mood disorders, anxiety disorders, sexual disorders, personality disorders, adjustment disorders, etc. Not all of these would affect a person so deeply as to render him or her incapable of marriage. Some of these disorders, however, are more prevalent than we would want to admit, and they have a far more destructive impact upon a person's ability to marry than once believed.

Let's reflect, for example, on what are called *personality disorders*. Any textbook in abnormal psychology would go into far greater detail than I intend here, but for our limited purposes, a brief description of some of these disorders might prove enlightening and may, in some way, describe the problems you have experienced in your own marriage.

We all have various personality traits: the ways we interact with others and with our world. We all have our ways of perceiving and understanding our own experiences and what they mean to us. We have our attitudes regarding all the persons, places, and things that make up our environment, and we interact with that environment. Some of our personality features make us lovable and others, to be honest, probably annoy even those closest to us. Begin with an honest admission: the biblical and ecclesial teaching that we are all flawed human beings in need of redemption is an undeniable fact. There are no perfect human beings.

But with that being said, there are those whose personalities are *inflexible* and *maladaptive*, thus impairing a person in his or her social relationships and often causing distress. "Inflexible" and "maladaptive" are sophisticated ways of saying that the way a person perceives and interacts with the world of reality *doesn't work* and the person *doesn't change*. At times the individual eventually understands that the problems are not with the world or with others, but within him/herself. At other times, these traits are *ego-dystonic*. In other words, the person is without a clue that he or she is acting in an abnormal way, hurting themselves, and having a truly negative impact on everyone else around. These patterns are usually lifelong though they become a real problem during adolescence and thereafter (cf. Wrenn, pp. 48-62).

Among the more serious of these afflictions is the *anti-social personality disorder*. Individuals suffering from this problem have a history, from about the age of 15 or so on, of truancy, fights, forcing others into sexual behavior against their will. They are unable to sustain a monogamous relationship, have no regard to the truth, are cruel to people and animals, steal and can't seem to keep the same job. They are unable to conform to social norms or lawful behavior, are impulsive, undependable, aggressive, and so on. They may not act in this fashion every single moment and they may not have all of these personality characteristics, but the pattern is there. This is more than mere emotional immaturity, although that is an element of the problem also to be sure. The type of relationships in which these persons are involved can be, and most of the time they are, destructive to the spouse and, of course, the children.

*Borderline personality disorder* is another example of a severe personality disorder which is the subject of a lot of psychological interest in our day. The full description is to be found in the D.S.M. III - R 301.83. One suffering from borderline personality disorder is a person who is prone to a "pervasive pattern of instability of mood, interpersonal relationships and self image." The "instability" is manifested for example in how the person tends to "over-idealize" the partner at one time and then will dramatically change and "denigrate" him/her before others. Such persons are unpredictable and impulsive in terms of spending money, sex, reckless driving, substance abuse, and so on. They tend toward emotional extremes. They can display intense anger in inappropriate circumstance, threaten suicide, complain of emptiness or boredom with life. They are unable to settle down and establish a self-image, sexual orientation, or career goals, and become paranoid about the possibility of being abandoned by others.

These are brief samples of two out of many personality disorders. Perhaps some of these character traits were present in your marriage. Perhaps there is a basis for an annulment of the marriage based on these disorders. You should speak with a priest in the tribunal.

In such cases of a psychological nature, there frequently is also present an indication of other more traditional grounds for Church annulment. It is not uncommon, for instance, to discover that the person with an anti-social personality disorder has no intention to give his or her spouse the right to acts which may lead to the conception of children. He or she may have no intention of remaining faithful. The decided absence of such elemental components of a valid marriage can only serve to further prove a case of invalidity.

What must be remembered is that often many serious types of issues dovetail with amazing frequency to create a solid case for a Church annulment of a marriage. Perhaps one element alone will not be sufficient to prove your case but, once examined, often more pervasive grounds for annulment are discovered. Unsurprisingly, while one ground alone might not suffice for the arguing of an annulment case, all the other indications for annulment which surface in a thorough marital investigation, taken together argue to its invalidity in Church Law.

## (E) GROSS IMMATURITY (CANON 1095)

When one speaks of immaturity, the usual thoughts conjured up are those of youthful abandon, whereby the immature are viewed as those who are of a young age. Clearly, age is not the issue here. Rather, the issue is the mental and emotional ability to meet the demands of responsible living in a way that indicates an overall personality stability.

In a thought-provoking article, "Immaturity, Maturity, and Christian Marriage," which appeared in Vol. 25 (1991) of *Studia Canonica* (the Canon Law Journal which is published out of St. Paul's University in Ottawa, Canada), Fr. Robert W. Guiry presents a working definition of maturity:

Maturity is, within *reasonable* limits, the age *appropriate* to the concordance of autonomous behavior, response, emotion, and cognition, in accord with the cultural, familial and gender milieu of the individual (p. 98).

*Reasonable* and *appropriate* are the essential concepts here. There has to be a reasonable ability to act as "one's own guide" (autonomous behavior) in a way which is appropriate to one's age, sex, family background and culture. The individual must be able to *respond* and not merely *react* to life with impulsivity. There must be some kind of emotional stability (cf. pp. 98-99). The author cites specific areas in a person's life that would give some kind of indication regarding their level of maturity: how they deal with money, sex, children, family and planning (p. 100).

Over a decade in this work has forced me to consider other issues as well. Richard Issel in his article, "Contemporary Marriage: A Psychologist's View," confirms my own experience, viz. that mature persons are not so completely absorbed in their own lives, problems, ways of thinking, feeling, or doing. They can separate what is truly important in life from what is trivial. They have meaningful values or goals with beliefs and actions which are for the most part consistent with those values. Mature individuals see their own role in what happens to them in life. All problems that are experienced are not always other people's fault. They can recognize their own limitations and are able to deal with their own and other persons' feelings.

From the opposite perspective, can one pinpoint some of the consistent or visible characteristics of the immature person. Such persons usually use poor judgment in fundamentally important matters affecting their own life or their contact with others. They would display egotistical behavior, a self-seeking, jealous, and perhaps even immoral approach to life and other people with whom they associate. They would show signs of emotional instability in varying degrees. These immature individuals have what we'll term a *non-social* (as opposed to an *anti-social*) personality disorder. They are hostile, easily show disgust and distrust of others. Such persons seek self-gratification. Like children, immature persons think of "self" first. Only what makes the "self" happy is considered.

The immature person very often ends up with a broken marriage, and yes, even a string of broken marriages. The grossly immature do tend to repeat their mistakes. I have had the sad experience of dealing with persons who have been involved in two or three broken marriages. When asked to describe the circum-stances of each, it becomes painfully clear that the patterns of problems are most often not merely similar but identical. If one were keeping a written "file" on each marriage, the only thing that would differentiate each case is the name of the spouse. And, of course, the problems are all and always the spouse's fault! These persons are flippant enough when single, but the worst indication of immaturity only surfaces once they plunge into the burdens and responsibilities of married life. They are ill-equipped to handle an intense interpersonal relationship of any kind, but most especially that demanded by a sharing of life and love with a spouse in marriage.

It is quite obvious what we mean here by gross immaturity. At times it will be a form of psychological disorder, but frequently it is not scientifically verifiable. The signs of immaturity are clear to any reasonable observer. A simple illustration: one may not have the medical or psychological expertise to make any determination about a person who decides to "show off" and race up a one-way street in the wrong direction driving blindfolded; however, to any reasonable person, such an action would surely evoke a response that the driver is *at least* immature, if not "crazy." From the standpoint of the jurisprudence of the Church, Fr. Guiry cites an annulment decision given at the Roman Rota on July 11, 1985. The Judges, in an *affirmative decision*, indicate that what we know as "affective immaturity" can arise from different "sources." The immaturity of "adolescence," for example, was noted as a source, as was a "personality disorder." Likewise an "immature characterological pattern existing in an adult age, notwithstanding the reaching of a chronological growth..." was cited as a source of such "affective immaturity" (cf. Guiry, p. 104, quoting a Rotal Decision *c.* Stankiewicz dated 7/11/85).

To have had the elements of gross immaturity present in a marriage is to have reason to believe that there is a possible basis for an annulment case. If you have been the unhappy party to a marriage in which your spouse was grossly immature, or if on reflection you can look back and recognize how grossly immature you were at the time of your marriage, then I would suggest you consult your tribunal.

To prove your case you will need at least *your testimony* and, hopefully, that of *your former spouse* as well (although this is frequently difficult when immaturity is involved, for the immature are seldom responsible enough to take a Church process seriously). You will also have to provide *witnesses* who would be in a position to describe first hand not only your marital situation, but also all of the aspects of your relationship with your spouse, even those prior to the marriage. What is examined are the signs of immaturity present all along. Finally, in several tribunals, a *psychological evaluation* may also be required. I might add at this time that often people become very defensive when the issue of a psychological evaluation is raised. The complaint is often heard: "But I didn't do anything wrong," or "I'm not the crazy one in this." We are not talking here about *blame*. Even if your former spouse were the most grossly immature and horrible person imaginable, very often the psychological evaluation of the person seeking the annulment provides a lot of insight into why you were so attracted to such a person. This is about truth, to be sure, but it may also have as an ancillary effect a "wake up call" to avoid that kind of relationship in the future. Whatever tack the tribunal in your diocese uses to help you prove your case, the best advice I can offer is for you to listen carefully, ask questions, learn about the subject, and cooperate with rather than fight those who are trying to help you.

By way of a footnote, it should be noted here that ignorance of what a marriage is or entails may lead to an invalid marriage. This is mentioned because the two, *ignorance and immaturity* frequently go together and, therefore, should be understood together. It has been the experience of tribunal judges that the whole issue of ignorance must be addressed when cases are processed under some form of psychological grounds.

## (F) HOMOSEXUALITY (CANON 1095, 3)

We hear a great deal of discussion these days regarding the homosexual and his or her relationship to society. Long a sexual attraction whose very mention conjured up revolting and disgusting thoughts and elicited quick denunciation, homosexuality is now treated and dealt with openly, without scorn. On the positive side, this is a welcome development in society, for the homosexual has a right to be treated as a human being and without prejudice or discrimination. There are still many unanswered questions about "sexual preference" and the "choice" of such a lifestyle. The *Diagnostic and Statistical Manual of Mental Disorders* no longer lists homosexuality *of itself* as a psychological anomaly. This text makes reference to those who feel discomfort with their homosexuality (D.S.M. III - R 302.90: "Sexual Disorder Not Otherwise Specified"), and mentions those who suffer "persistent and marked distress about their sexual orientation." In the world of psychiatry the issue would appear to no longer be homosexuality itself but rather whether or not the homosexual accepts his or her orientation. Obviously there are many dimensions to this issue. Our interest here is in how this condition impinges on the validity of marriage.

While some avowed homosexuals seek out "marriage" with someone of the same sex, it is not infrequent that many marry persons of the opposite sex. Thus we have a distinction made between the avowed homosexual (one who accepts his sexual orientation) and the so-called "closet" homosexual who usually ends up marrying and whose case frequently winds up in a Church court for annulment. Why these individuals marry is an open question. Perhaps they reason that marriage will "cover up" their "problem." These persons oftentimes are not true homosexuals properly so-called, but rather are more bisexual than homosexual. By bisexual is meant one who is attracted to members of both sexes. Consequently the bisexual can carry on a sexual relationship with one of the opposite sex (say, for instance, in marriage) and at the same time engage in a sexual relationship with one of the same sex. At times homosexuals will (or can) only relate sexually to a member of the same sex. The true homosexual is frequently repulsed by any thought of relating to the opposite sex sexually (much the same revulsion a heterosexual experiences at the thought of relating sexually to someone of the same sex).

It should be pointed out that under certain, unusually extreme or specific situations, both men and women who are heterosexual have been known to engage in sexual relationships with persons of the same sex. Some instances of these situations would be: prisons, institutions, military service, camps, or any living situation where contact with the opposite sex is extremely limited for any number of reasons. These persons are not genuine homosexuals but rather engage in homosexual activity as a means of releasing sexual tension from unique circumstances or pressure situations.

In the first edition of his work on annulments, Fr. Wrenn cited Donald Webster Cory's work, *The Homosexual in America*, in which Cory posits twelve reasons why a homosexual marries:

1. Desire for children
2. Need for permanent family relationship
3. Inability to create permanent relationship with companion or lover
4. Fear of loneliness of older years
5. Desire or hope to escape from homosexual life
6. Deep affection for someone
7. Latency or repression of homosexuality
8. Hope of finding companionship in marriage; disappointment at inability to find it outside of marriage
9. Desire to create the facade of married life and hope to find protection against gossip and its concomitant evils
10. Aspiration for economic and social gain
11. Desire to please family
12. Inability or unwillingness to take strong stand in order to put an end to drift toward marriage

These twelve reasons are recorded here so that the reader might more clearly understand not only *that* homosexuals marry, but *why* they might do so.

Regarding the possible annulment of a marriage entered into by a homosexual, it should be noted that this is viewed specifically in the new canon 1095, #3: a person's inability to assume the obligations of marriage. One might also have sufficient evidence to argue that the homosexual's motivation for marriage was so defective that he also incurred other grounds for annulment which might dovetail with homosexuality itself as a ground for nullity. The situation will be identified by the tribunal investigating the nullity of a marriage when homosexuality is involved. Depending upon what is learned, the Church court might then decide to process the case on one or more of the traditional grounds which will have become evident through the course of its analysis of the marriage in question.

Any person who finds himself/herself enmeshed in a marriage of this sort should submit their case to the tribunal. The chances are very good that the Church will grant an annulment. The evidence needed to prove the case will vary, depending on circumstances and the cooperation of the parties involved. It is best to leave the question of *necessary proofs* to the tribunal handling your case, rather than for this author to suggest to you the evidence necessary in any given case and thereby mislead you. Your case may not fit the general pattern and, therefore, might require further or not as many proofs as the case may be.

## (G) SIMULATING THE SACRAMENT OF MATRIMONY

This ground was mentioned briefly in the initial section of this chapter. "Simulation" of the sacrament of marriage means that one enters marriage *not* with the intention of entering a lifelong loving conjugal union, but only to fulfill some obligation or to gain something extrinsic to marriage. Now this is a simplification. Simulation is a complex ground for annulment. For our limited purposes it will suffice just to outline the basic meaning of simulation. Canon 1101 of the Code of Church Law specifies the meaning: If either or both of the persons through "a positive act of the will" excludes either marriage itself, or some essential element, or some essential property, then that marriage is null and void.

For instance, Philip marries Roberta in order to give a name to the child she conceived out of wedlock. Philip has no intention of remaining in the married state with Roberta after the ceremony. He is only doing what he perceives to be the "right thing to do." Remember it is not Philip's notion that he has the right to leave the marriage or he thinks about leaving the marriage that makes the marriage null. He must have positively intended to leave this marriage even though he is promising to marry "until death do us part" during the ceremony.

Another example might be: Kathleen marries Michael in order to get his money. Michael is wealthy or stands to inherit wealth soon. Kathleen marries so as to "get in on the deal." She has no intention of living her life with Michael in spite of taking marriage vows. Her only intent is to have his money. This is simulation of the sacrament.

Still another case would be marriage to escape military service. This is no longer a case which comes up in the United States since there is no longer an obligatory military service, but in the past, when the draft was still on, it was not unknown for men to marry to avoid being drafted into the military. If this were the sole reason for marriage, and if the person had no intention of assuming both the personal and procreational obligations of marriage as a sacrament and conjugal covenant, the marriage would be invalid.

This is not the easiest case to prove. It is rare that a person would explicitly "by a positive act of the will" intend one thing while saying words that mean or promise something else. Also another difficulty is that to positively exclude something is *not* the same thing as not including something. To positively *ex*clude fidelity when I marry is not the same this as not *in*cluding fidelity. However, jurisprudence in the interpretation and application of law has taught that people can *implicitly show* what they really intend. Fr. Wrenn in his 5th edition of *Annulments* lists three examples:

> — if a person positively excludes the right to cohabitation, then of course he or she is implicitly excluding the right to a partnership of life and therefore marriage itself.
> — if a person goes through marriage for extraneous reasons

which have nothing to do with marriage itself, this implicitly would show simulation.

— if a person substituted his own idea of marriage, then he or she enters something different from marriage (pp. 89-93).

*Partial Simulation: Defective Intention Against Fidelity*

There are three "traditional" grounds of nullity: an intention against fidelity; an intention against a permanent union; an intention against having children. These three venerable grounds for annulment have as their basis a type of consent which is either conditional or at least certainly defective. This person does not intend to deliver on one or other of the marital promises. The person places an intention to exclude one of the essential components necessary for true conjugal life.

In the case of *intention against fidelity*, the party entering marriage excludes the right of the spouse to an exclusive sexually conjugal relationship. The right to fidelity is a fundamental one. If for example, Gene marries with the intention of continuing a sexual relationship with some other woman, makes this an extension of the marriage contract so to speak, and intends to deny to his future spouse her right to his being faithful to her, the marriage is null. He has not intended to give his wife the right to his fidelity. This does *not* include the situation of the wife or husband having an extra-marital affair that develops after several years into the marriage. Nor does it include any "mid-life crisis" which is "solved" by "finding oneself" which usually means finding adultery! While such behavior may indicate (possibly) that there are other grounds for annulment, given the overall context of the marriage relationship to date, it would not suffice to render a marriage null and void on the grounds of a defective intention against fidelity made when one professed marriage vows. In this case, as with all marital breakdowns, the tribunal should be consulted.

The quality of proofs needed to support this ground for

annulment is highly complex. To cite all the possible forms of evidence would only serve to confuse and discourage the reader. As with all petitions for annulment, the quality and quantity of evidence required to prove your case will be determined by the tribunal.

*Partial Simulation: Defective Intention Against Having Children*

The Church has always held the view that children are intrinsic to the meaning and purpose of marriage and that marriage must be open to the procreation and generation of offspring. This does not affect those persons who, because of a quirk of nature, or perhaps some other physical cause (accident) are not able to procreate. The Church is rather referring to those cases in which the right to have children is denied by an act of the will: "I do not wish to have children" or "I will not have a child," or "I never intended to raise or beget a family."

It frequently happens today that a couple will marry having decided beforehand to put off having children until they are settled, which usually translates into being more or less financially secure. This means that they generally enter marriage with the express intention of practicing birth control (we will presume that the methods used are those approved by the Church and, hence, in no way reprehensible) until such time as they are ready or prepared to start raising a family. This is all well and good and essentially a matter of conscience, but the familiar sequence of events generally follows an identifiable pattern: everything starts out just fine and moves along with both parties working to secure their "fortune" or to insure minimum financial difficulties. Then, after some time — generally a couple of years — one of the parties to the marriage starts thinking about raising a family. So the one party asks the other party for a child. The other party does not agree. He or she would like to wait still longer, perhaps a few more years. The spouse reluctantly agrees to wait but not three or more years. Time passes and the request is made again. Once more the same answer — no.

By this time the marriage is shaky and before long it ends in divorce with the aggrieved spouse claiming that the other party would not have children. What has happened is simple. The putting off of children for an agreed upon time was part of the marriage contract. When the one party requested the fulfilling of the agreement it was denied and, therefore, the right had been denied, since it is obvious that the aggrieved spouse married with a view to raising a family. If he or she had known that this would not be, the marriage would never have taken place.

We could cite dozens of possible examples, and they would all be variations on the theme. But this is a very complex ground and one which tribunals try to avoid when possible. The Church has maintained in its interpretation of the law that there is a real difference between *never giving* the right to children as opposed to merely *misusing that right*. A person may initially have the proper intention, but later on, as circumstances in life change, the person then changes his or her mind. Perhaps greed and love for financial security (which was never an issue or intention before marriage) changes the person's attitude about a family. Perhaps there are already *other* problems in the marriage, and one spouse simply realizes that to bring children into a bad marriage will merely further complicate and make worse what is already bad! What matters is what the person actually intended at the time of the marriage. And this can be a very difficult thing to prove.

If the absence of children plays a crucial, or better, an essential role in the breakup of the marriage, the tribunal should be consulted. Even if an annulment cannot be obtained on this ground of defective intention against children, it is solidly probable that the willful absence of children could indicate yet other probable grounds for resolution of a problem by a Church court. The complexity of this type of case makes the listing here of all the categories of evidence needed in order to prove a case, unrealistic and superfluous. The best approach is to take your case to the local diocesan tribunal, where they will indicate to you what proofs are required by Church law.

*Partial Simulation: Defective Intention Against Permanence*

Living in a society characterized by a pervading sense of impermanence, it is reasonable to assume that "marriage for life" will be duly affected by this social attitude. Marriage is always one of the casualties listed when impermanence and frivolity rampage society. It is not unreasonable to presume that today a "divorce mentality" is foraging across America. This situation carries with it numerous liabilities for everyone and makes the entering into marriage a somewhat precarious and, at times, perilous undertaking. Clearly, this cultural mentality produces serious matters for consideration by Church courts.

When one enters a marriage with a defective intention against the permanence or perpetuity of the marriage bond, that person enters into an invalid union. For instance, "I will marry you now but on some future date, I intend to leave and marry someone else." Perhaps more realistically, "I consent to marry you, but if this marriage becomes unhappy, I intend to divorce you so I can be happy." The person who marries must give consent to the right to a lasting marriage. It is not merely the case of "believing in" or "not believing in" divorce. It is not merely the case of believing that one has the right to divorce even at will. It is a matter of knowing that marriage is a permanent union, but I have no intention of marrying under such circumstances.

The nature of perpetuity and permanence is such that it enters into the basic definition of what marriage is in its essence. To intend to enter marriage with a view to the right to divorce at some later time is not to give one's spouse the right to a perpetual union. One's outlook can be such that he or she believes in permanent marriage, *only* if the situation works out — otherwise divorce is in order. This strikes at the heart of our Christian understanding of the nature of marriage and, therefore, given the above attitude a marriage contracted with such a prior intention can be annulled.

If you have become involved in such a marriage, please contact your tribunal for assistance. While the grounds here spoken of can be most complicated and intricate, nevertheless, this does not mean that you will be unable to prove your case. Particular notice should be paid to this ground today since numerous young marriages are being contracted under these conditions outlined. There is no surefire guarantee against marrying someone with a defective intention. However, if you suspect that your spouse never intended to remain married to you for life, bring your story to the Church court. It is the only way you will ever know for certain about your chance or prospects for a Church annulment.

### (H) FORCE AND FEAR (CANON 1103)

A marriage is "forced" upon a person by someone in a position to apply pressure (parent, superior, etc.) and the pressure must lead to great fear on the one being forced to marry. This means that the party is so fearful of the possible consequences of non-compliance that he or she submits to the pressure and marries.

The ground of force and fear is extremely difficult to prove. Owing to the complex nature of this ground for annulment, we seldom have cases today processed under this heading for nullity. However, force and fear is an issue which does demand mention in a book such as this and, therefore, ought to at least be properly understood.

The most frequent example of this type of situation involves a premarital pregnancy. This situation is probably not nearly as common today as in the past due to the availability of birth control devices and the early level of sexual awareness. Still, it is not uncommon that once pregnant a girl will either find strong pressures being applied to her to marry "or else" (and the "or else" usually produces fear). The boy might find himself in a similar situation when pressures to marry the girl he "got into trouble" become so intense that he fears the possible consequences. This is the "classic" case; however, it cannot always be proven that, in a particular premarital pregnancy situation force and fear were present to a sufficient degree to render a marriage invalid. It happens that the case presented ends up being tried on some other grounds which can more easily be proven.

The best thing is to submit one's case to the tribunal and have the tribunal determine if a case exists and can be proven from the existing facts and the evidence available. If you have been involved in a similar situation, perhaps your marriage can be annulled. It is certainly worth the effort to find out.

## (i) CONDITIONAL MARRIAGE

It sometimes happens that parties to the union place certain *conditions* upon the outcome of the marriage. These are made prior to the ceremony and have to do with some future situation or circumstance which radically affects the validity of the marriage. The placing of conditions upon marriage may be more widespread a practice today than one would suspect. With the cultural climate encouraging the pursuit of happiness and self-fulfillment as an absolute right, it is little wonder that some persons may attach conditions upon their entering a lifelong union with another person, which union could be the bearer of great unhappiness. In countries outside the United Stated conditional marriages have long been a problem plaguing the Church. These marriages were usually contracted in order to secure an inheritance, or royal lineage, land, or perhaps political domination, not to mention the run of the mill conditions which are of a more universal character.

Now that everyone is sufficiently confused, here are some examples of what the Church would mean by a *conditional marriage* or a marriage contracted with conditions placed upon it:

— I will or intend to marry John *provided that* he stops drinking heavily.
— I will or intend to marry Maria, *only if* she is a faithful member of the Catholic Church.

— I intend to marry Kathy *provided* she will never take drugs.

— I will marry Tiffany *only if* she is heterosexual, fertile, wealthy, genetically sound, etc.

— I intend to marry Louis *as long as* he's never been married or ever gotten a girl pregnant before.

These and any number of conditions placed on a marriage make the question of validity a complicated one. One of the major problems is that people usually don't talk in such a way. Even when they think that way, they are not of a mind to share that information except under unusual circumstances (e.g., when drunk). The law of the Church has been simplified when it comes to conditions: if a person enters a marriage and has placed a condition about the future, the marriage is null. If the condition is about some past or present event, the validity of the marriage depends on whether the condition was met.

As with reference to other grounds for annulment, the way in which the condition is placed, the intention invoked, and the requirement for proof are highly complicated areas for study. We can only scratch the surface here. What is singularly important to remember is that there is a ground for annulment based upon a condition placed upon it by one of the parties to the marriage. Therefore, if your marriage is one involving a breakup, perhaps based upon non-fulfillment of a condition, then the tribunal can be of service to you and help you attempt to cull the evidence for proving your case.

## (J) FRAUD OR DECEIT (CANON 1098)

A new ground of nullity has been added to the 1983 Code of Church Law. Scholars and Jurists will argue whether this ground ought to apply to any marriage or only those marriages which have taken place since the new code. It seems pointless to enter that debate. Among the purposes of any legal system is to protect members of the community. This certainly applies to ecclesial law as well. This new ground would seem to have as its purpose to protect a person from being misled into a marriage by deception or misrepresentation. This is not a question of a lack of knowledge about a person simply because of wrong assumptions, foolish presumptions, or the immaturity of youth. There must be, for lack of better words a *deceiver* and a *victim*.

As the law is written a person must have been misled into marriage by the act of fraud about a quality in the other person. Logically one supposes that this would be a "bad" quality. What is essential is that the quality can "gravely" disturb conjugal life, and that the "victim" was specifically led into this marriage by the "deceiver" through his act of fraud. If there had been no act of fraud, there would never have been a marriage. If the "victim" had known the truth, there would have been no marriage.

One specific example that the law itself foresees is the case of hidden sterility. Suppose Kirk is sterile from some disease or accident, and knows this. But he does not tell Christa this, and she consents to marry him without a clue about this. If she had known the truth, she would never have married him. And he withheld that information precisely because he knew that she would never marry him under such circumstances.

People have an astonishing capacity for deception. In order to get what is desired, in this case marriage, some persons will try to impress their partners with wonderful tales about themselves that simply are not true. Sometimes this is a symptom of a personality disorder which underlies the lying and the cheating; sometimes it is a sign of fear. Alice has a serious disease, AIDS for example, and knows that to tell Roger of this will doom her to a life of more loneliness. So she withholds this information from him. One can imagine that this quality is grave and by its very nature will disturb their married life.

If this situation has a familiar ring to it, then again I strongly suggest you consult the tribunal. They will assist you in proving your case. As usual, the veracity of testimony and perhaps some witnesses will be sufficient to prove your case. In any event, the Church court will do all it can to assist you in obtaining an annulment on this ground or some other ground in the area of defect of consent.


## CONCLUSION

The foregoing has been an attempt to enlighten the reading public on the various grounds for annulment in the Church today, as well as briefly explaining the meaning and function of tribunals in the Church. To be sure, many who read this book will recognize in their own conjugal life elements which could pass for possible invalidity. However caution must be taken when reading and assessing a marriage, whether it be yours or that of a friend or relative. Caution is demanded. Not every marriage can be declared null. Frequently the grounds upon which a case might be built cannot be supported with the evidence necessary to grant an affirmative decision.

Yet it is today's experience, particularly in America, that most of those petitioning for a Church annulment usually obtain a favorable decision. As we mentioned earlier, this must not lead to false optimism since disappointment in this area can be profound and bitter. While the Church has grown in its overall understanding of what marriage is and in what the necessary elements demanded for validity consist, nevertheless, the Church is not in the business of running "divorce mills" or "annulment factories." No one can hope to slip a case by the tribunal with little or no effort or cooperation and *especially* honesty. The Church has always, and will continue to scrupulously monitor marriage and annulment, for family life must be preserved, fostered and strengthened.

The Church realizes that many people become enmeshed in marriages which were never valid. It is to these facts the tribunal ministers and for those faithful that the Church courts were founded. This is not to say that marriage work is the only work for tribunals, but only that, essentially, at least today, most of a tribunal's workday, week and year is taken up with annulment proceedings.

There are those voices, both in and outside the Church, which would have you believe that there is no need for tribunals. All that need be done, they say, is to declare the union dead and start again. To these we respond, "You are sadly mistaken." For while the Church courts still have a great deal to do and much further development is necessary in order to more adequately meet the needs of our faithful and insure swift justice, this does not argue for the uselessness of tribunal structures. People need official approval for remarriage. This need exists apart from the Church's laws. It is a basic psychological need to have official approbation for action which seems somehow to be viscerally out of order. That is to say, people marry in order to stay together for life, raise a family and share love. When the ideal fails, it brings upon one a feeling of insecurity which leads to self-doubt and guilt. What the advocates of "carte blanche" separation and divorce without Church intervention fail to realize is that their philosophy is psychologically hollow and produces more guilt and insecurity than if the person faced up to the dilemma in the Church.

For too long now the average person has known nothing of the breakthrough in the annulment procedure. Most still believe that, once married, however dreadful or perhaps invalid, nothing can be done to help them after the union has come apart. The purpose of this book is to bring both laity and clergy up to date on just where annulments now stand and the rights of people to a hearing. Not to know is not to be helped.

May those who find themselves in a broken marriage, upon reading this book, be inspired to have their lives set aright in the Church through a tribunal review of their case. May those reading this book who have relatives and friends involved in marital failure pass along the information contained herein. Then perhaps others in need of help may find in the Church's courts the justice they thought themselves denied, and in finding justice, discover the rewards of perseverance and peace.

# APPENDIX

## 1. THE TYPE OF FORMS OR "PAPERWORK" INVOLVED

There is not a person who isn't somehow aware that this process involves "paperwork." Therefore I thought that the reader might want to preview some of the *types of forms* that are used. I have chosen the outlines of a particular diocese. Obviously the exact questions, the order in which they are placed, or any particular emphasis will vary from place to place. The diocesan tribunal where you reside may use forms similar to these. On the other hand, they may look quite different.

However it is obvious that all tribunals, in their attempt to minister in this juridical area are going to focus on the same issues, no matter the exact wording or order of their questions. So what is important is that you look over this section and prepare yourself for the kind of reflection and soul searching that this process is going to require from you. Perhaps this is the first time that you will have been forced to face issues that stem from your own family and childhood, your years of dating, or the marriage itself.

The *first set* I have listed involves the *preliminary* or *initial interview* that will take place either in the local parish with a priest/ deacon/parish minister or at the tribunal office with a person who works with individuals who are interested in beginning a case. Be familiar with the terminology. The person *seeking the annulment* is called the *Petitioner*. That person's former spouse is referred to as the *Respondent*. Any diocesan tribunal with which I have worked or whose forms I have studied tries to avoid the civil law terms of "Plaintiff" or "Defendant." After all, you are not putting your former spouse "on trial." It is the *marriage* that is being examined. Are there reasons why this *marriage* is not valid: either because of some defect in the "form" (the ceremony), or because of the existence of some Church impediment that was never dispensed, or because of some defect of consent. This is not a process that has as its intent to *blame* either you or your former spouse. Hopefully the end result will be peace of conscience for yourself and a return to full participation in the sacramental life of the Church — especially for those who are divorced and have entered a "second" marriage "outside the Church."

It is the *ideal* that the tribunal staff member of the parish minister fill out this *Interview Sheet* with you. Too often, as in most aspects of life, the ideal cannot be achieved. If you must fill out such initial forms on your own, please take the time to be accurate.

Biographical questions about Petitioner and Respondent are rather simple. Yet in the years I have been in this assignment, I am forever reminded that people know, care to know, or care to recall so little about one another. Sometimes what a person does not know about one's former spouse (like the birthday of the man or woman with whom you have lived for 22 years) speaks volumes about communication or sensitivity within a relationship.

A question is often asked: Does the *Respondent* have to cooperate in this process? Must his or her "permission" be given before one can present a case to a Church court? The answer is very simple: Any person whose marriage has failed and wishes a Church court to examine that marriage has the *right* to do so! The "permission" of the other party is *not* required for you to present a case. It is a sad fact of tribunal life that more often than not, the Respondent either ignores letters sent asking for cooperation, or in some outlandish (often vulgar) response categorically refuses to participate. In these instances (which are the *majority*) of cases, a person may certainly present a marriage case for examination for a potential Church annulment.

Now that being said, let me also state two other points that are crucial. A person has a *right to present a case*. That does *not* mean that there is a "right" to an annulment. An affirmative decision in your case will depend on whether there are grounds for an annulment and whether those grounds are proven beyond a reasonable doubt. There is no such thing as an automatic annulment. The point I am making is simply this: one cannot assume that, merely by presenting a case, an annulment will automatically be granted. Your case must be proven. But you need neither the permission nor the cooperation of your former spouse to at least present a case.

There is a second very important issue: the other party does have a *right to participate* if he or she wishes to do so. While your former spouse has no right to prevent you from presenting a case to the Church and asking for a decision about the validity of your marriage, he or she does have the right to present their "side" or perspective. An annulment process is not a "secret trial" by some form of ecclesiastical K.G.B. The Respondent might even object and object strongly to the possibility of a Church annulment, and their objections might be for honest reasons. They may be for completely foolish reasons. Those reasons might be prompted by nothing more than sheer spite and meanness. Whatever the case, a person has the right to participate. That does not mean that a person's former spouse has control over the case or that by stating an "objection" or "bad feeling" about the process, they have any right to prevent you from presenting your case for a decision.

What this does mean in a very practical sense is that the tribunal has both a legal and moral obligation to invite your former spouse to participate to the extent that he or she wishes to do so. They may give testimony. They may present witnesses to give testimony. They might even raise all sorts of objections. In other words they have parallel rights to any right that you have. Therefore they must be invited to participate, *not by you* but by the priest judge who is handling your case. Information about a Petitioner, such as a new married name, your present address, whether there are any children from a second marriage, etc. is *never* given out. Your right to privacy in these matters is respected. But it is *never* permitted to try to put a condition on this process: I want to "go for an annulment" but I don't want my former wife involved. That is not possible.

Therefore you will notice that information about that Respondent is requested on the initial interview sheet. This includes name (full name, including any possible new married name if the Respondent is a woman and she is in a new marriage), address, etc. You *must* be as truthful as possible in giving this information. If you don't know where the Respondent presently lives, please make every honest effort to find out. Is there contact with his/her family that still resides at a known address? What was the Respondent's last known address? If there are children from your marriage, do they have contact with this other parent? Are there friends who can help you out? Do you have contact through the Social Security system? If, after an honest search, the Respondent cannot be found then, of course, you still maintain the right to present a case. One can never be held to the "impossible." If that person is no longer in the area and everyone has lost touch, then this fact of life is accepted, and your case does move on. To withhold that information from the tribunal and lie about not knowing the Respondent's whereabouts is taken as so serious that in Church Law, when the lie is discovered, and one would be amazed how such lies do come back to haunt a person, the entire annulment process is invalidated, i.e., it ceases to exist, you have nothing. A person would have to start all over again except that now the person has lost all credibility after having lied about the Respondent's whereabouts. So I cannot stress this point enough: be as accurate as you are able in giving the Church court the address of your former spouse. As you will note, the form we use asks for the exact same biographical data about the Respondent.

The next section of questions will usually ask you to focus on the relationship with your former spouse. When did you meet? How long did you date each other? Was this a smooth and happy relationship or a rocky one filled with breakups even at this time. Did you live together before marriage? Was there a pregnancy involved at the time? These questions give fundamental background information about the time you were dating, the courtship.

The final section will ask you some information about your married life: how long you lived together; number of children; when the separation(s) occurred; the grounds for divorce, etc. Regarding one's legal status as a divorced person, please keep these *truths* in mind insofar as much "fiction" seems to exist in the popular mind:

a) Simply because a Catholic is divorced does not of itself mean that he/she cannot receive the sacraments! The real issue is whether a Catholic has tried to enter a *new marriage*. It is *divorce and remarriage* that becomes the problem. Civil divorce *of itself* does not change a Catholic's spiritual status within the Faith Community. One is not excluded from receiving the sacraments when one is divorced but not in another marriage.

b) The grounds for divorce *usually* play no role in the annulment process. A marriage will not be declared null and void because one's spouse was unfaithful, there was a lack of compatibility, or any such civil "reason" for divorce. On several occasions I have heard that so-and-so was granted an annulment because "she was unfaithful" or "he didn't want to have children"! These issues may indeed be raised, but as you have already read in the chapter on the grounds of nullity, you can appreciate that simple declarative sentences like the ones mentioned hardly prove a case by themselves.

I'd like to make mention of one final point: notice at the conclusion of this preliminary interview form, information is requested whether there might be any *language* problems or any *financial* problems that might interfere with a person's right to have their marriage examined by the tribunal. There is a long-standing *rumor* — based upon no fact whatsoever — that annulments cost thousands of dollars and that you must have "friends in high places" to obtain an annulment. This could not be further from the truth. The next time you hear stories about so-and-so was told by "some priest" that it will cost "thousands of dollars," ask for the name of the priest! You will find that the person cannot come up with a name. In all my years in this work, I have yet to get one actual name! It's always "some priest." These stories seem to have a life of their own, handed down from generation to generation without anyone taking the time to challenge them.

Please read over this initial form, and then we shall examine the type of questionnaire which you will most likely be using to assist you in giving the tribunal the kind of information needed to process your case.

*Do You Have a Case?*

# INTERVIEW REPORT SHEET

— PLEASE PRINT —

_____   _____
Man's Last Name           Woman's Maiden Name

_____
Woman's current legal name: Maiden, Married,
Newly Married

**PETITIONER:**_____

      First      Middle Initial   Last  (Woman's Maiden Name)

ADDRESS:_____

TELEPHONES:  Home ( ) _____ Business ( ) _____

DATE OF BIRTH: _____ PLACE OF BIRTH_____

FATHER: _____ HIS RELIGION: _____ Living or Dead _____

MOTHER: _____ HER RELIGION: _____ Living or Dead_____

PETITIONER'S RELIGION: _____

HIGHEST EDUCATION COMPLETED: _____

OCCUPATIONS: Now _____ On Wedding Day_____

DATE OF BAPTISM: _____ PLACE: _____

_____

**RESPONDENT:**_____

      First      Middle Initial   Last  (Woman's Maiden Name)

ADDRESS:_____

TELEPHONES:  Home ( )_____ Business ( )_____

DATE OF BIRTH:_____ PLACE OF BIRTH: _____

FATHER: _____ HIS RELIGION: _____ Living or Dead _____

MOTHER: _____ HER RELIGION: _____ Living or Dead _____

PETITIONER'S RELIGION: _____

HIGHEST EDUCATION COMPLETED: _____

OCCUPATIONS: Now _____ On Wedding Day _____

DATE OF BAPTISM: _____ PLACE: _____

_____

**MARRIAGE INFORMATION:**
FIRST MARRIAGE FOR PETITIONER? _____ RESPONDENT? _____
APPROXIMATE MEETING DATE: _____
LENGTH OF COURTSHIP: _____
DATE OF ENGAGEMENT: _____
LENGTH OF ENGAGEMENT: _____
DID COUPLE LIVE TOGETHER BEFORE MARRIAGE? _____
    HOW LONG? _____
BREAKUPS BEFORE MARRIAGE? _____
    HOW MANY? _____ HOW LONG? _____
PREGNANCY BEFORE MARRIAGE? _____
DATE OF WEDDING:_____ PLACE OF WEDDING: _____
NUMBER OF CHILDREN: _____ WERE THEY BAPTIZED? _____

**BREAKUP:**
HOW LONG DID COUPLE LIVE TOGETHER? _____
SEPARATIONS OTHER THAN THE FINAL? _____
    HOW MANY? _____ HOW LONG? _____
APPROXIMATE DATE OF FINAL SEPARATION: _____
DATE OF LEGAL SEPARATION, IF ANY: _____
DATE OF DIVORCE OR CIVIL ANNULMENT: _____
    WHICH? _____
WHO SOUGHT DIVORCE/CIVIL ANNULMENT, PETITIONER OR
    RESPONDENT? _____
WHERE? _____ DECREE #:_____
DATE OF DECREE: _____ GROUNDS: _____
HAS PETITIONER REMARRIED? _____ DATE: _____
HAS THE PETITIONER EVER BEGUN AN ANNULMENT PROCEDURE
    BEFORE? _____
IF YES, WHERE? _____
NAME OF INTERVIEWER/ADVOCATE_____
PARISH - TOWN _____
DATE OF INITIAL INTERVIEW_____
IS LANGUAGE ASSISTANCE NECESSARY IN THIS CASE?_____
WILL FINANCES BE A PROBLEM IN THIS CASE? _____

The most important (and probably the most painful) of all the "work" that must be done is the telling of *your* story. I highlight that single essential word: *your*. This is the one aspect of the entire process that no other human person can do for you. No one can relive your experiences. No one can fully appreciate your memories, both joyful and agonizing. While there are those in this ministry who will be most happy to assist you in every possible manner, ultimately there must come that moment when the story of your life must be unfolded, and the only person qualified to do that is *you*.

I have been told countless times that dealing with the type of autobiographical questionnaire, like the one we are about to present, is or can be both upsetting and liberating. To face one's own human frailty, fallibility, and foolishness is a difficult task. A person might look upon one's own family of origin and find that, yes, very often the problems of the home ("the sins of the parents," as it were) do come back to haunt us. At other times it brings a person pain to know that, although he or she was the product of a loving and caring environment with hard working and decent parents, one's own adolescent arrogance and the "immaturity of youth" brought such pain to one's own family and to one's own self. Self-reflection can bring freedom, for as Jesus Himself taught us: "The truth shall set you free." But the truth of self-revelation will all too often remind us of how much we do not know, did not see, failed to love and appreciate, etc.

Please examine this questionnaire carefully. Most tribunals use a form that is in some way analogous to this. You'll note that there are three primary areas which are examined: one's *family background*, the *courtship* or dating years (months/weeks), and then finally the *marriage* itself.

Whenever asked what is the single most important thing a person should do when dealing with this questionnaire, my answer is a straightforward, simple sentence: "Be truthful." While it may seem just a bit absurd to even raise this issue, all too often I find myself dealing with persons who even at this time are attempting to "get something" for themselves and, if they can avoid honesty in the process, all the better. I have at times had to remind persons that they are under oath when they testify. It is not just a little awkward when you are speaking with a person and trying to assist, and in the face of responses which contradict information you have already been told, the person smiles somewhat sheepishly and says: "Oh, you mean you know about that!" If this process is not based upon truth, it is meaningless in the sight of God and, no matter what a Church court might decree, if a decision is not based on the truth, it is not only "legally" (in Church Law) without any merit, it is just another lie. Have persons been "smart enough" to "fool" a Church court? I suspect so. But ultimately when those persons, as we all must, stand before the Lord to render an account of their lives, all the ecclesiastical "paperwork" in the universe won't matter, will it?

The next bit of advice I would offer: *be as thorough as you can.* One word answers to these types of questions rarely help. As you start putting together your thoughts, ask yourself "why" such and such happened. Understanding the *why* of a situation is almost as important as understanding *what* actually happened. Try to be accurate with *date and times* if this is possible. Much can be learned about why there may have been problems in a relationship depending upon how long persons may have known one another. A two-year courtship should reveal more insight about an impending marriage relationship than a two week dating relationship.

Another piece of advice comes freely but is far more of a challenge to put into practice: *try not to focus your attention so much on your former spouse.* Deal with the questions as they are. Many times I have read through these statements which are little more than thinly veiled diatribes against one's former husband or wife (or the infamous mother-in-law)! Let this be an exercise in self-manifestation: what did I live through? Why did I do as I did? What should I have seen or listened to back then? Why was I blinded by "love"? Giving the tribunal a list of all of the physical, intellectual, moral, spiritual, sexual, vocational failures of your former spouse does not of itself address the issues that the tribunal must examine. One particular case several years ago struck this writer when he opened the envelope and found that the Petitioner had disregarded the questions entirely and had written an essay entitled: "_____'s Problems as a Wife." This misses the point although it revealed volumes about the gentleman himself!

A final admonition I usually make whenever I give any sort of presentation about the annulment process. Don't be afraid to deal with issues not listed on the questionnaire. In other words, whenever it is necessary, go beyond the prepared questions. Every person's life is unique, and a general questionnaire cannot possibly cover every possible issue that affects a person's decision to marry. If a woman were living in a home where from the age of 14 she was being raped by a male family member, and this issue obviously colored her decision to marry at age 17 to any person who'd show her a "way out of there," that is an issue which obviously plays a very crucial role in her decision to marry. Whether there is any question about sexual abuse in the home or not, the issue must be addressed.

Examine these questions to see how a person's life is looked at. They cover far more than the marriage itself. A failed matrimonial relationship is *not* the issue that needs to be proven. It is *why either or both of the parties were not ready or able to be married* in the first place. A person's capacity for a relationship, not the failed deeds and broken promises are the primary focus of a Church court.

# PETITIONER'S OUTLINE

| | |
|---|---|
| Man's Name | Woman's Maiden Name |

## *Family Background*

1. What was it like to grow up in your family? (Were you raised by both parents? How many children in the family? What was your relationship to your parents as a child, then as a teenager? What was your parents' relationship with each other? Was it a close loving family or not?)
2. Were there any specific problems at home that had an effect on you in later life? (E.g., alcoholism, drug abuse, child abuse, rape, gambling, divorce or separation.) How did this affect you?
3. Do you think your parents gave you a good model of what a marriage should be? Why/why not? Did you want your marriage to be like theirs? Why/why not?
4. At what age did you become interested in members of the opposite sex and begin to date? Was this the same time as your peers/friends or later/earlier? Until you met your former spouse, did you date regularly? Were you popular at school or work?

## *Courtship*

1. When and under what circumstances did you meet your former spouse, and how soon afterward did you begin to date him/her on a steady basis?
2. What initially attracted you to him/her? How long did the courtship actually last?
3. Were there any serious fights or breakups during the courtship? What were they about? *How many* and *how often*? Did anyone advise you to break up for good?

4. Compare the family background of your former spouse to your own. In what ways were they similar families and in what ways different.

5. Was there any objection to your dating your former spouse on the part of your parents, other family members or friends? Who objected and why? What was your response to their objections?

6. Who proposed marriage? What circumstances led to the proposal? Was the proposal accepted immediately? If not, why not?

7. Did both families approve? If not, why not?

8. Were either of you pressured into marriage? Please explain.

9. Did you discuss matters like being faithful to each other, having children, marriage is forever? If not, why not?

10. Did the priest/minister give you any reasons why you should not be getting married? What were they?

11. In what ways do you believe that you were not ready to marry?

12. In what ways do you believe that your former spouse was not ready for marriage?

13. Were you looking forward to getting married or were you having second thoughts? With whom did you discuss your second thoughts?

## Married Life

1. Were there any problems at the *rehearsal*, the *ceremony* itself, or at the *reception*? What were they?

2. Were there any problems on the *honeymoon*? What were they?

3. Was your marriage consummated on the *wedding night*? If not, was there any problem? When was the marriage consummated?

4. Was your sexual relationship ever a problem? If so, what were the problems?

5. Could you speak frankly with each other about any sexual problems? Did you seek counseling?
6. What would your former spouse's complaints about you be?
7. When did communication between the two of you become a problem? What were the particular areas of difficulty?
8. When did the serious problems in your marriage begin? Did you or anyone else recognize them? What were they?
9. Had the above problems been present during courtship? Did you notice them then? Did anyone else warn you of them?
10. Were there any specific problems with homosexuality, substance abuse, crime, gambling, child abuse, physical violence? On your part or the spouse's?
11. Any problems with overspending on either part?
12. Was there any indication of general irresponsibility?
13. Were either of you *impulsive, selfish,* or *ungrateful* on a regular basis? Please give an example or two.
14. Did your relationship with your family change after marriage? If so, how?
15. What events led to the final breakup?

The final type of "paperwork" with which the reader might wish to become familiar is the type of questionnaire that many diocesan tribunals use when gathering testimony from *witnesses.* A word about "witness testimony" is necessary. Many times I have had persons ready to "give up" on this process because they indicate, "But nobody knew what the problems in the marriage were," or "I never let anyone know what I was living through." Also there is the fundamental question: "Why do I have to have witnesses?"

To the question of the necessity of witnesses there is both a "canonical" response as well as one from common sense. From the point of view of Church Law, whenever the issue being examined is one that affects the "public good" (and marriage as an institution and a sacrament is not merely a private affair between the two persons but does affect the entire Christian community) the word of the person alone is not enough for what one might call *full* or *complete proof*. The word of the person seeking an annulment is of course considered something of a proof or evidence, but it must be evaluated and weighed with any other circumstances that would affect the question being examined (which in this case is whether a person was truly ready and capable for marriage). For the record this principle in Church Law is found in canon 1536, #2.

There is also a very simple and logical reason why witnesses are required. The annulment process is *not* a counseling process. It is not sacramental confession. Of course, some very private and often painful issues are raised during this procedure, but in and of itself this is a juridical process. A person is approaching the Church and asking for justice: that his or her marriage be examined and, if the reality is that this marriage was null and void, then to have it declared such. But the person does, in effect, *want* something. It isn't sinful or evil to want something. But it is a fact: a person does want a specific result. Anyone could say anything to get that result if he or she wished to do so. Whenever I have given talks in parishes about this process, often the objection is immediately raised: Why would anyone try to lie about their life "just to get an annulment"? To be honest, I don't have an answer to that question, but it does happen. People do have the capacity for deceit when they want to obtain something. Now of course if an annulment were so obtained by such lies or fraud, in the long term it would be spiritually meaningless. So obviously one of the main purposes of any witness is simply to be able to declare (either at a session when oral testimony is given or perhaps by questionnaire) that yes, I know that this or that issue which the Petitioner is raising is true. I can verify that this happened. I know that this occurred.

There is another value to witness testimony that only a Judge ever appreciates because he respects the privacy and the trust of given witnesses. Very often it is their experience that a person seeking the annulment is really without much insight into his or her own life. We've all heard the cliche that people are "blinded by love." They can also be blinded by pain, loneliness, bitterness, and so forth. On more than one occasion, I have had a Petitioner swear that she came from a perfect and close family with no problems at all. Her brother later testifies that his sister lives in a dream world, that their father was an abusive alcoholic, and that his sister could not wait to get out of the home by any means at all, which is why at 16 she became pregnant and married. I have had a gentleman swear that his former wife completely changed her personality the day after the wedding, and that she had never even looked at a drug much less abused them during the time they dated. I have then had witnesses explain how the woman had had a reputation in the neighborhood for both promiscuity and drug abuse, but this young man would not listen to their admonitions. And this goes on and on. So very often witnesses not only confirm what a person claims. On occasion they add truthful information that either the Petitioner does not know or cannot face because it is too painful.

*Who should be asked* to act as a witness in your case? First of all, think about the questionnaire that you will have to fill out as a Petitioner. There are general areas of your life that are going to be looked at. There is your own *family background* as well as what might be known of the *family background of your former spouse.* There is that most important time while you were *dating.* Finally, of course, there is the *marriage* itself. If you could simply focus on those four areas and then ask yourself who might be able to verify or know some or all of the information you are about to reveal in one, several, or all of those areas. Don't believe that a witness must know everything about everything. Very few of us really know or under-stand all the dimensions or experiences of one another. But you might find that in your own life there are categories of persons who could assist you. Your *parents* and *siblings* are the first choice. Surely they can verify what you are about to indicate regarding your growing-up years. You may have *close friends* who may really know nothing of your experiences at home but know more about your courtship than your parents (presuming that few of us ever go out on dates with our parents). You may even have *another* set of friends or relatives who know more about the problems within the marriage itself.

Please look over the following example of a "witness questionnaire." Ask yourself *who* are the people that *know me* and what I have lived through? Were there any persons who had strong feelings (usually negative but unexpressed) at the time I was going to marry? Were there those who tried to make me see what I just was not ready or willing to look at? Were there people who did try to talk me out of marriage at the time? Perhaps even the priest of the parish (if he is still alive or remembers the events) might be a possible witness. Very often priests have very strong "feelings" about whether this or that person is really ready for marriage, but they cannot act on what they merely "feel."

When a person might ask you what he or she is "supposed to say," tell them simply to be honest. They are not there to condemn either you or your former spouse. Nor are they there to propose you for sainthood. Tell them to be as straight-forward as they are able. Sometimes they may be asked to recall problems or events. Most judges have no problems with a person who has spoken to a potential witness and helped them to remember a common experience. That is far different from putting words in another person's mouth or simply repeating "hearsay" evidence. I've often asked a witness why he or she was selected by the Petitioner. All too often I've heard: "I don't know." Talk with your people. This process is far too important for you.

In some dioceses, the style of the particular office may dictate that a witness questionnaire by itself is all that will be asked of them. In other dioceses, that witness may have to give testimony orally either in person, by telephone, through a parish priest in the area where they live (since rarely do all our friends or family members still reside in the same area), or in any way that the Judge will determine. Please warn them in advance that filling out the questionnaire may not be the only thing asked of them. I cannot overly emphasize the role these persons play in your annulment case.

# QUESTIONNAIRE FOR POTENTIAL WITNESS IN ANNULMENT PROCEEDING

CASE: _____ _____

PETITIONER (If woman, maiden name)    RESPONDENT (Former spouse)

In an annulment proceeding, the Church is examining whether two people were *truly ready for marriage* as well as the *cause of the failure* of the marriage. We ask you to treat the *negative aspects of this marriage* as well as *any reasons why either or both parties should NEVER HAVE MARRIED in the first place*. Be as candid and thorough as possible; a simple "yes" or "no" to the questions posed does not yield much information. It would expedite the process if your responses were typed or printed in ink. Please use the back of this or a separate sheet of paper for your answers to the numbered questions. Your help as a witness is indispensable and deeply appreciated by all concerned. The information you supply to the Tribunal will be held in strict confidence. We ask that you reciprocate this confidentiality and not discuss with *or* show your statement to either of the parties or other witnesses involved in the case.

## PLEASE PRINT YOUR NAME AND ADDRESS

YOUR FULL NAME: _____

YOUR CURRENT MAILING ADDRESS: _____

_____

YOUR TELEPHONE NUMBER: _____

YOUR DATE OF BIRTH: _____

YOUR RELATIONSHIP TO THE PARTIES: _____

1. How long have you known them?
2. Please describe the family atmosphere of *each* of the parties as they were growing up and *before marriage*. Detail any problems.

112

3. Can you describe the personalities of *each* person *before marriage*?
4. Were there any features that would make either of them ill-suited for marriage? Did the other party notice or accept these features?
5. Do you feel that they *both* were ready to accept the responsibilities of marriage? *Why*?
6. Did anything unusual happen during courtship: fights, breakups, unfaithfulness, addictions, etc.?
7. Did the marriage meet with the approval of the families? Did you approve? Why?
8. Were there any problems at the wedding, the reception, or the honeymoon?
9. When did the problems in the marriage begin? What were they? Did they exist even before the marriage? When did you first notice? How did you find out?
10. What brought about the final breakup of the marriage? Were you surprised that the marriage ended? *Why*?
11. Is there any other information that you feel the Tribunal ought to be made aware of?

PLEASE NOTE: This is a preliminary paper which gives the Tribunal an idea of what information you know. You may be requested to offer *sworn testimony* sometime in the future should this case become a *formal case* and it is felt that your testimony can help the case.

I do understand this and would be willing to give further testimony as needed.

Signature: _____ Date: _____

There is another source of proof or evidence that might be helpful for your case. We can group this type of proof under the name *documentation*. If a person has undergone any counseling (and especially if counseling touched upon issues of family background or experiences during the time your were dating your former spouse), then perhaps a report from that counselor (psychologist, psychiatrist, psychiatric social worker, etc.) might be helpful for your case. At that time when you were dealing with these issues, you might have touched on some of the types of questions that a Church court needs to examine. Questions about a person's willingness, need, readiness, understanding about, or maturity for marriage may have been raised. If that is the case, then please let the priest or other tribunal staff member with whom you are working be aware of the existence of such counseling reports.

There are three admonitions I would offer about this as a source of evidence for your case. First of all, please be aware that there may be limits as to how long any professional in the "helping" fields might be allowed to keep records. It may be that after a number of years, those records have been destroyed. Still it is worth the expense of a phone call to the clinic, office, or hospital to find out. Secondly, the reader will have noticed that I specifically did not mention *marriage counseling*. The reason I am hesitant about this comes from lived experience. Many times records are requested from marriage counselors, and the reports always focus on the crisis of the moment that was destroying the marriage relationship. Of itself this is not helpful. It may give added weight to a person's account of why the marriage failed. But this type of report by itself usually does not give the tribunal the information about family background, psychological makeup, and so on, that is needed. On occasion this does occur so it is always worth at least the attempt to secure such a record, but the end result from my experience is not always helpful. Finally, I would remind the reader that if the counseling sessions involved both you and your former spouse, if there is any essential information about your former spouse that could be revealed, it cannot be given to the tribunal without the permission of your former husband or wife. This is often very difficult to obtain as one might imagine. So please keep these potential problems in mind.

Another often overlooked source of evidence could be *written material* from the time of your marriage. When questions arise about a person's freedom to marry, or one's intent to marry for life (as opposed to "I'll give this a shot but if it doesn't work, I'm walking"), perhaps there are letters which a person wrote to one's parents or friends that still exist. Did a person write down one's fears, expectations, intentions in a diary? In the course of meeting with the parish priest, was there some problem during the time of preparation for marriage, and did he leave a letter or some kind of notation in the marriage file? Sometimes the material used in the various pre-matrimonial programs have been kept, and little clues about serious potential problems were already being ignored. On more than one packet from a certain Pre-Cana Workbook I have read words to the effect that when asked to "fill in the blank" to the statement, "I don't always care for you when...," the woman had written: "...you drink all the time and slap me around." Here was a wonderful statement about the drinking behavior of the gentleman *before* they married. What made this all the more curious, in one particular case, was the insistence that alcohol was "never" a problem beforehand. He only began drinking on the honeymoon for the first time ever! So documents can be most helpful for a case.

## 2. PREPARING COUPLES FOR MARRIAGE: A NEW PERSPECTIVE*

There is much discussion these days concerning the preparation of couples for their future marital union. Both at the provincial level and, to a larger but more general extent, at the level of professional societies, such as the Canon Law Society of America, the arresting question of how and to what extent the Church must properly prepare young persons for marriage is being seriously considered.

The pre-marital investigation which the Church, in theory, takes most seriously has been conducted by way of custom in a very *pro forma* manner. This is due in large part to the many outdated and unrealistic questions proposed in the pre-nuptial questionnaire. While some questions are to the point and the proper documentation indispensable, others are of dubious value at best. The time has come to reevaluate and reformulate our pre-nuptial investigation process and to begin asking some very pertinent questions which reflect the cultural condition in America.

Before presenting those areas of investigation which are in need of discussion and elucidation, let us set the context for our analysis by way of some background.

Perhaps the overriding consideration when attempting a discussion on the causes of marital failure and its possible prevention by way of preparation is to mark out the root cause — that of ignorance. Most marital failures result from ignorance and its offshoots: fear and distrust. The less we know about someone the greater the probability for our future alienation from him. Our distance from another is directly proportional to our ignorance of him as a person: ignorance of his beliefs and hopes; his dreams and difficulties; his joys and sorrows; his past mistakes and present interests.

## Who Am I Marrying?

It seems that in America, people generally marry with less knowledge of their partner and with less understanding of marriage than they possess when purchasing something in a store. The experts in the fields of social psychology relate to us that their studies indicate almost one-half of all marriages last year will end in personal and social disaster. In California the percentages are even higher. If America is indeed the unhappy leader in the field of marital discord, as these figures would seem to indicate, then the acceptable time for doing something about this condition is upon us.

Some unsettling and arresting questions remain unresolved: What is wrong with a system of values and attitudes that will allow the richest, most educated nation on earth the liberty of basking in so dubious an honor? What has gone awry in a society which allows its people the lamentable joy of impermanence? Why does America paint so ugly a picture of so beautiful a relationship? Why do people so quickly ask out of that for which they worked so long getting into? Is life as absurd as all this seems to demonstrate? Is love a fleeting experience which defines itself in terms of a temporary commitment?

Perhaps if marriage were to be made more difficult to get into, instead of getting out of, it would drive home the seriousness of the commitment involved. This posture might give one pause before jumping at the chance to enter a relationship that terminates only in death. What if we required a certain degree of mutual knowledge as a prerequisite for entering upon a lifelong commitment, would there then be the number of dissolutions we presently see? For instance, if couples planning marriage were obliged to investigate their motives for marrying each other and the obligations ensuing from such a relationship, it is solidly probable that many would choose not to marry this particular partner.

Current studies cite the following reasons for much of the trouble marriages encounter: (1) The pressures of modern society. (2) The urban crisis. (3) The nuclear age and its corollaries. (4) The overriding mood of permissiveness. (5) The smashing of traditional mores. (6) Contemporary financial burdens, and so on. Now, while most professional counselors insist that such a battery of problems may and can aggravate already existing marital difficulties, they equally insist that they are not the root causes of marital discord. Instead we find these realities being dragged into existing relationships as so much excess baggage. This should not astonish us; it has always been a fact of life.

Marriage today is no more joyless than it has ever been. What creates today's rise in unhappiness and discontent is people's increasing unwillingness to settle for such a sad state of affairs.

People quite dissatisfied with their marriages are less likely today to be long-suffering. Of course through all of this the recurring problem of personal ignorance stands alone as the root cause of joylessness. The intensity of joylessness is proportional to the rise in misunderstanding and lack of proper communication in any given marriage. Ignorance spawns misunderstanding which is the result of lost communication. Ignorance of each other's views on life and love and a variety of related topics is key to marital trouble. Ignorance breeds fear and distrust which are the usual causes for separation and divorce.

How does a couple cancel such ignorance? People cancel ignorance by informing one another concerning those areas of life and love which touch directly upon their married lives and the hopes they possess for a realizable future. Let's discuss some of the practical, gutsy categories that affect marriages but are seldom touched upon in current matrimonial preparation. Let us perhaps attach these questions in the manner of an agenda to the current pre-nuptial questionnaire:

### Is Money the Problem?

His salary: What is the annual income of your fiance? Does it serve to satisfy his needs at present and will it (given increments) serve to allow fulfillment of his hopes and dreams for your future together? But more importantly, are you, his bride-to-be, really content to live on that salary and the level of social status which it creates, and do so for the rest of your life? Are you really content with this? Will his financial status allow you to function socially as you feel you must and still be capable of educating your children, and at the same time live in relative comfort? Do you plan to work? Do you like to work? Do you want him to place as much importance on your career as he expects you to place on his? What about the children if both of you are working? Honesty here is a grave necessity.

What if, at some future date, your spouse is called upon to

support his or her parents. Will you accept this policy with the warmth and love that gave it birth or rather will this eat away at your feelings and needs concerning "cutting loose those apron strings," therefore spawning resentment: "I wish he or she were as concerned for me!"?

*The In-Laws*: Suppose the wife is extraordinarily close to her parents and requires constant visitation in order to be "true" to her love for them. Or perhaps the husband's parents are the ones who insist upon his continual and frequent visitation. Can you cope with this situation? Has it been discussed and agreed upon? What if one of the wife's parents (or the husband's parents as the case may be) dies; will either of you refuse to allow the living parent to move in with you? How strongly do you feel about this prospect?

## What Priorities Prevail?

Now suppose, for instance, that the fiancee visits her widowed mother two or three times weekly and has done so for a number of years running. Or possibly she still lives at home. Both she and her mother require this presence. How will this situation affect the prospects of moving to a new location away from the mother? For example, her finance's job requires such a move and he is opposed to her mother's moving along with them. What priorities are operative here? Is compromise essential? If so, how far does one go in compromising on such matters?

*Abortion*: Here lies a potential battlefield; also a classic example of how not knowing something about one's future spouse can be disastrous. What if the fiancee has had an abortion and fails to tell her boyfriend prior to the marriage. She kept this information back from him out of embarrassment and shame. Or perhaps her boyfriend has indicated his disgust and revulsion for anyone who would have an abortion. Then later he finds out that his wife has had one. This can quickly precipitate an end to the marriage.

When a couple contemplating marriage begins to talk seriously of the future, their respective stands on this matter of abortion should be very clear. If either of the two feels that abortion is an acceptable means to the elimination of an unwanted pregnancy and the other, following the teaching of the Church, is vehemently opposed to such a thought, then the seeds for future turmoil exist and chances are they could be sown. Sharp discord on this issue would make a second look at this marriage's prospects imperative.

*Residence*: This question is an important one, and while it is discussed by most couples, oftentimes it is not fully investigated. The couple about to be married agree that city "Z" will be their residence. Here is where they will settle and it is here where their children will grow up. However, the husband's (or perhaps the wife's) employment may require, at some future moment after the couple is already settled, moving to another state or even to another country. Will your initial agreement on the location of residence still remain the same? Have some feelings and values remained unexpressed prior to marriage? It would appear that an agreement which both feel they can live with in tranquility and unreservedly must be entered into before the marriage. Nothing else will assure a minimum of difficulty when and if such a problem should arise in the future.

*Religious Beliefs*: If agreement cannot be reached along these lines then, like politics, discussion about this area of life can prove to be distressing at best. If one of the parties is religious, can he or she tolerate the irreligious lifestyle of the other? Will their divergent points of view affect the religious upbringing of the children? Will either interfere with the other's conscience as it touches upon the question of religion? Artificial birth control, for example, as a means for regulating the size of one's family, is condemned by the Church as contrary to human dignity and the nature of the marital act. When one partner accepts the Church's teaching in this area and the other does not, all kinds of problems can arise. Will the disbelieving partner ridicule the beliefs of the other? If so, can this be done to such an extent that their love becomes permanently wounded? How will all of this affect the children?

If religion is an integral part of life, as experience clearly indicates, then its relationship to a marriage is certainly a question that needs to be addressed and addressed fully.

*The Working Wife*: It is almost a given in society today that the wife will work, either out of sheer necessity or because she wants to pursue her own career. If the woman decides, after the birth of her child, that she will return to work, what effect will this position have on the marriage if the husband insists upon her being home with the kids? Since so many of today's women are college graduates and therefore presumably looking for an outlet by which to exercise their knowledge and skill, how will their perspective spouses view their interest in a career outside the home? It can also happen that a woman wants to stay home and raise the kids but the financial situation is such that she is practically obliged to go to work and, at times to accept a job which she does not like so that she can attend to her children at least part time. Has this been discussed and accepted with tranquility and good grace? If these matters are not settled definitively prior to contracting marriage, then serious crises are inevitable.

### Should We Adopt?

*Adoption*: Take this case, for example: both parties want to have children but for some reason they cannot seem to have them. What then? Assuming that, after consultation with a physician (or psychologist) the couple discovers that one or the other is sterile, how will the marriage hold up? No one, of course, knows for certain. But what is sure is that the couple who thought it necessary to discuss this vital question will be able to deal with this situation more rationally and with greater tranquility.

The question of adoption then arises. She wants children but he refuses to "take in somebody else's child." "If we can't have our own then we'll have none." The tension is apparent. Once again, unless this question has been cleared up before marriage, the possibility of disaster resulting from this problem becomes a reality for the couple. Since sterility can be visited upon any marriage at any time, the adoption question simply must be agreed upon before a contract takes place. Not to do so will insure a state of ignorance regarding the feelings of the other partner, and such ignorance can return to haunt a marriage and perhaps even destroy it altogether. The question: If sterility becomes a reality for us, will we adopt?

## Vacations Are Important

*Vacation and Family Recreation*: Ignorance within this area of marital life is not to be taken lightly. Most working men and women live from vacation to vacation. They save frugally from week to week and plan intensely for vacation as the year speeds along its appointed course. Vacation seems to instill within a marriage some sort of sanity and joy. It offers a well-deserved break for those who have worked hard in the salt mines of life. It isn't a panacea for all problems, but it certainly enables one to see the difficulties in a far more comfortable and relaxed light.

Now, everyone has his own peculiar ideas about how a vacation should be spent, or exactly what a vacation is or even should be. Given such variety of personal opinion, and given the context of marriage, there flows a need for necessary flexibility on the part of the partners that allows for mutual agreement. Aside from the difficulty of coordinating such a venture, what problems are likely to result from ignorance in the area of one's vacation?

*Young Children*: Should young children be dragged, say, to the shore where every year countless toddlers are badly sunburned and require hospitalization? Or should they be taken on long automobile trips, and how do you keep them occupied and reasonably happy while you're getting where you're going? Young children have a way of determining the place for your vacation. This must be discussed by the couple and agreed upon ahead of time. What will we do for our vacations while the children are still young?

*Type of Vacation*: What is a vacation for one person can be hell for another. What is a vacation for a wife might not be a vacation for the husband. What is a vacation for the children isn't a vacation at all for the parents. How does a resident grandmother or grandfather affect your family's vacation plans? These and other vital questions should be dealt with by the couple, ideally, even perhaps if only hypothetically, before the marriage. What exactly is each partner looking for from his or her vacation? How will both of their needs best be served? If a vacation is not a vacation for all, chances are it is a vacation for none.

### Hobby or Hubby?

*Hobbies*: Another vital outlet for recreation and relaxation is a hobby. It allows and provides a means for creativity and personal satisfaction. The sad fact is that some hobbies work against a marriage rather than support it. Some hobbies demand more time and, I dare say, more love than is given to one's spouse. Some hobbies are not compatible with another living under the same roof. They have prerequisite conditions necessary for their proper fulfillment. In many cases the spouse may be directly affected and therefore should be agreeable to the hobby. The needs of the spouse must be taken into account when considering a prospective hobby. If, for instance, a particular wife requires the loving presence of her husband and her husband's hobby is hunting and fishing, one which takes him away frequently (oftentimes during holiday seasons), then perhaps his hobby could be the cause of resentment. It is likely, therefore, that she will belittle his hobby. If this hobby is extremely important to him (perhaps overly so) her belittling might ignite a full-scale marital war.

*Eliminate Confusion*: The same applies with regard to her hobbies. It seems that if trouble is to be avoided, one's spouse must be in some way involved with the other's hobby, however remotely that might be. Ignorance and insensitivity here, coupled with a dose of non-communication, is a source for numerous aggravations and discord.

I have attempted to outline just some of the less-talked-about areas within married life which can lead to domestic discord if not

properly understood and reasoned out together. Very often es-
trangement and alienation begin with confusion over these simple
elements that constitute the vitality of marriage because they
require the life-giving ingredient — communication. Adequate
understanding in the aforementioned areas of married life will help
sustain a lasting personal relationship. The motives for which one
enters marriage should be scrupulously analyzed and reflected upon
before attempting a long-term commitment. Nothing but honesty
will suffice.

    * With minor modifications to reflect the situation in the '90's,
this text appeared as an article published in *Homiletic and Pastoral
Review* (Vol. LXV, no. 4, January 1975). It is reprinted here with
permission of the publisher.

## 3. INSTRUCTION BEFORE MARRIAGE:
## THE RESPONSIBILITY OF THE CHURCH

    In one sense this section title is misleading. The reality of so
many broken marriages has led for reform of pre-marriage "programs." This is not a new cry. The inadequacy of present day Pre-
Cana or other such diocesan programs, rules, structures, and so on,
appears an observation of any pastor who is dedicated to his
community and takes his responsibility of stewardship and service
seriously. It seems that most newly ordained priests complain about
pre-marriage programs ahead of just about every other complaint.
So many men and women who have had to undergo the annulment
process have commented that they wish a substantive marriage
preparation course existed "in their time."

    While I have no disagreement with those comments, I must
confess that preparation immediately before marriage would not
seem to be the answer to the ever-climbing rate of broken unions.
Courses and programs cannot fix what is already broken, and if a
person is not truly ready for or capable of marriage, no course or
lecture will change that reality. The older I grow, the more I

appreciate the many dimensions to St. Paul's insight that *knowledge* of the law does not bring salvation. While he was addressing a completely different issue, his insight remains true: to have knowledge or information (law, etc.) does not of itself bring understanding or commitment.

The revised Code of Canon Law devotes an entire section to *Pastoral Care and What Must Precede Celebration of Marriage.* Great emphasis is placed on a pastor's responsibility to make sure that preparation for marriage doesn't begin the day a couple makes an appointment to schedule their wedding. In my opinion the present day canon 1064 presents rather well the varied dimensions of marriage preparation:

Pastors of souls are obliged to see to it that their own ecclesial community furnishes the Christian faithful assistance so that the matrimonial state is maintained in a Christian spirit and makes progress toward perfection. This assistance is especially to be furnished through:

1° preaching, catechesis adapted to minors, youths and adults and even the use of the media of social communications so that through these means the Christian faithful may be instructed concerning the meaning of Christian marriage and the duty of Christian spouses and parents;

2° personal preparation for entering marriage so that through such preparation the parties may be disposed toward the holiness and duties of their new state;

3° a fruitful liturgical celebration of marriage clarifying that the spouses signify and share in that mystery of unity and fruitful love that exists between Christ and the Church;

4° assistance furnished to those already married so that, while faithfully maintaining and protecting the conjugal covenant, they may day by day come to lead holier and fuller lives in their families.

Just as one cannot legislate morality, one cannot legislate either attitude or commitment. Anyone reading the above cited "law" of our Church would have to admit that there is a strong underlying conviction that preparation for marriage cannot begin merely with the meetings a parish priest would have with the couple. The attitude is one of facing a strong need to present marriage as the focus of teaching, preaching, writing, conversations, workshops, and so forth in our educational programs. The focus should be appropriate to the age and maturity of the persons. The first time a young man or woman hears about the value and command of fidelity, let us say, should not be when the question is raised during the pre-marriage interview. The values, needs, responsibilities, obligations, hopes and joys, sorrows and pain, hard work and happiness of married life has to be something that our youth are exposed to from their earliest years in the classroom, from the pulpit, the media, and from a multitude of other sources. Believing that any one program is going to change a person's mind about marriage after the reception hall has been rented, the honeymoon is planned, and the hormones are raging is simply, in my opinion, unrealistic.

One also notices that in "law" value is placed on *post* marriage pastoral care. How many parishes are equipped and committed to care for persons who are living their marriage. Obviously programs like *Marriage Encounter* would meet this need. There is also the need for various counseling programs to assist couples in crisis. Can this be done on the parish level? Is this the work for priests all by themselves? What role will the laity play in this particular need and ministry. I have often wondered whether persons who have undergone the hurt and pain of a broken marriage and who have taken advantage of the annulment process with its demand that one reflect on the "why" of this tragedy might just be in a marvelous position to assist the local parish community. Those persons might be a most valuable resource because of their lived experiences. Again I would share my concern: any program will only be as effective as those who present it are committed to its success and those who are taking part in it have an open mind and heart and truly wish to learn, grow, and perhaps even rethink their upcoming wedding!

Back in December of 1981, Pope John Paul II issued a document (an Apostolic Exhortation) which is his teaching and reflection on the results of the Synod of Bishops which met in Rome the previous year. This work, *Familiaris Consortio*, addresses "the role of the Christian family in the modern world." Once again the need for preparation for marriage was stressed. Section #66 is devoted to the long-range goals and responsibilities of marriage preparation. *Remote preparation* begins within the home and family of the child. The family must be the environment where all true human values are taught. This is where "character formation" begins. The family must be the place where the ability to form interpersonal and social relationships is nurtured. Parenthood is nothing less than a monumental responsibility. *Proximate preparation* is the pastor's responsibility in that, in a variety of ways, he provides an appropriate catechesis for his parishioners on marriage, sexuality and morality and oversees a review of this material with the couple in preparation for their wedding. Finally *immediate preparation* for marriage is, of course, also mentioned.

I was struck by one sentence which to me again indicates the need for total Church commitment to this issue of trying as best we can to prepare young people for marriage: "The Christian family and the whole of the ecclesial community should feel involved in the different phases in the preparation for marriage which has been described only in their broad outlines." This is a work that is so desperately needed, and it is up to all of us, as members of the Church, to assume this responsibility. Only when this begins to occur will we even begin to make any headway to deal with the issue of broken marriages, broken promises, and broken lives.

## 4. CANON LAW'S STRUCTURE-CRISIS: THE VALUE OF LAW

Human structures, whether political or ecclesiastical, always seem to have been characterized by a "built-in" reluctance to change or to accommodate themselves in the face of newly evolving cultural patterns. Therefore, when values and behavior patterns reflect new ways of perceiving old realities, institutions ordinarily determine that their existence is threatened and react accordingly. The avant-garde usually completes the polarization of issues around which the crisis is revolving simply by challenging the older and more established perspective, which the institution reflects, with its own brilliant and highly suspect vision. In the presentation of new ideas, an avant-garde group frequently tends to dismiss the existing institution as "hopelessly outdated," an implicit accusation that the structure is inherently *incapable* of the desired modifications. The threatened institution on the other hand tends to consider the new vision as radical, "far-out," and therefore impossible to be assimilated. The establishment and the avant-garde seldom trust each other sufficiently to do the obvious: acknowledge the aspects of enduring validity which characterize the former, while assimilating the more relevant, and perhaps more truthful, expressions of permanent values which bring the latter into periodic existence.

The aforementioned structure-crisis exists today in Canon Law. The 20th century Church has become, over centuries of development, a highly sophisticated assembly of believers. Such refined development necessitates the proper subordinated role of the Church Law within its institutional framework precisely in order to maintain that stability which will lend credibility to the Church's overall mission of bringing the light of the Gospel to all nations. Such an exalted goal cannot be achieved by burying one's head in the sand and refusing to see the essential need for Church order in the form of appropriate legislation. Neither is one justified in pointing the finger at glaring insufficiencies in our present Code of Law and then attempting to "solve" the problem by a call to abolish the structure of law totally from the everyday life of the Church. This unwarranted and utterly simplistic "solution" cannot be based on some vague appeal to the "simple" structure of the Church in the first centuries of development together with the claim that such a primitive Church knew no legal system such as we have today. Of course it didn't! But neither did the Church know the structural development then that manifests its presence to the world today. As a matter of fact, the primitive Church did sanction a Church order, and it did, most assuredly, invoke human prescriptions to regulate in an orderly way the lives of Church members.

In its ethical understanding of the Gospel, the Roman Church has always proposed the ideal for its members. In the past this idealism usually afforded even hardened critics of the Church an opportunity to voice sentiments of admiration. Today, however, the phenomenon has made its appearance on the Church scene that not only doubts the usefulness of maintaining an ideal expression of the Gospel but even questions the validity of such proposals. One might presume that such rejection of Christian ideals is largely the result of a current obsession in many quarters of the post-conciliar Church to address the world in terms that are relevant to, supposedly, the world's understanding of itself. Some go even further and suggest that if the Church is not speaking to the world with an effective degree of relevance, the fault belongs with the Church which, they advise, should be corrected, even at the expense of Christian idealism. This view, unfortunately for those Christians who expound it, cannot be reconciled with either scriptural or theological expressions of the Church's divine mission to reconcile an alienated world to God, through the death and resurrection of Christ. It is the revelation of Christ that judges earthly values and assigns to them a validity proportionate to Christian existence. Life in Christ can never be made to hinge on conformity to a value system previously unassessed in the light of God's redemptive activity on behalf of humankind.

The Church must continue, therefore, to preach and uphold Christian life formulated according to its ideal expression. At the same time it must strive to assist each member to attain the realization of that ideal through a charitable assimilation of the frail human condition to the saving likeness of Christ. The Church cannot afford to settle for anything less than Christ's vision of marriage, regardless of any amount of outside pressure to abandon, however slightly, such a vision in the name of "relevance." The Church will thus remain faithful to the Word of God, even in the face of warranted legal criticism directed to the human ecclesiastical expression of that very ideal so highly prized.

## IN SUMMARY

An appeal must be made to our Christian people themselves to strive vigorously for a new awareness on their part that maturity of faith is vitally necessary to bring sacramental marriage into being and sustain it. We can reform structures, but we must at the same time renew ourselves also. A crucial part of that authentic personal renewal will necessarily consist in a reaffirmation of faith in the absolute indissolubility of a true Christian marriage, precisely for what such a sacred reality means and stands for. The reform of Canon Law itself, a constantly developing theological awareness into the deeper mysteries of sacramental marriage, the simplification of procedural law in order to more quickly, more justly, and more charitably expedite the process of annulment, and the evolution of broader grounds for annulment, are encouraging signs of a living and relevant Church seeking to correct the inadequacies of the past.

But even with the actual realization of these reform measures, the men and women who profess a faith in Jesus Christ and who are, for that reason, adopted children of the Father, will nevertheless be called upon by Christ to affirm for themselves in their own lives a sacred belief in the enduring nature of marriage in the Lord, a belief which can never be challenged without at the same time challenging the very Word of God upon which it rests: "What God has joined together, let no man separate." If Christian spouses choose to live in a sacramental marriage, then they elect to make of their union a permanent manifestation of Christ's glorious victimhood to an incredulous world. A genuine reform of matrimonial law and procedures ultimately derives its real justification and sense of purpose in aiding Christians to achieve this vision of marriage, ancient in our Christian heritage, but ever new in bringing a world striving for true love to that divine fulfillment.

# SOME OF THE WORKS CITED
# IN THIS BOOK

DOOGAN, Hugh F., Ed. *Catholic Tribunals: Marriage Annulment and Dissolution.* Newtown, NSW, Australia: E.J. Dwyer (Australia) PTY Ltd., 1990, 433 p.

GUIRY, Robert W. "Immaturity, Maturity, and Christian Marriage," in *Studia Canonica.* 25 (1991), pp. 93-114.

ISSEL, Richard P. "Contemporary Marriage: A Psychologist's View," in *Canon Law Society of America: Proceedings of the 43rd Annual Convention.* Washington, D.C.: C.L.S.A., 1982, pp. 84-94.

ORSY, Ladislas. *Marriage in Canon Law.* Wilmington, DE: Michael Glazier, 1986, 327 p.

SIEGLE, Bernard A. *Marriage According to the New Code of Canon Law.* New York: Alba House, 1986, 297 p.

WRENN, Lawrence G. *Annulments* (5th Revised Edition). Washington, D.C.: C.L.S.A., 1988, 174 p.

# SOME OF THE WORKS CITED IN THIS BOOK

...

# A SELECT BIBLIOGRAPHY

The following no way pretends to be a complete bibliography. However, I do believe that these books and articles (which can be found at Catholic bookstores or libraries) would give any reader a good variety of material upon which to reflect.

BOOKS

BASSETT, W. and HUIZING, P., Eds. *The Future of Christian Marriage*. (Concilium, Vol. 87), NY: The Seabury Press, 1973, 155 p.

BASSETT, W. and HUIZING, P. *Judgment in the Church*. (Concilium, Vol. 107), New York: The Seabury Press, 1977, 114 p.

DOOGAN, Hush, Ed. *Catholic Tribunals: Marriage, Annulment and Dissolution*. Newton, Australia: E.J. Dwyer, PTY Ltd., 1990, 433 p.

GRAMUNT, Ignatius, et al. *Canons and Commentaries on Marriage*. Collegeville, MN: The Liturgical Press, 1987.

HUDSON, J. Edward. *Handbook for Marriage and Nullity Cases*. Ottawa: St. Paul University Press, 1976, 172 p.

HUELS, John M. *The Pastoral Companion: A Canon Law Handbook for Catholic Ministry*. Chicago, IL: Franciscan Herald Press, 1986, (esp. "Marriage"), pp. 157-261.

LIPTAK, David Q. *The New Code and the Sacraments*. Vol. I, Lake Worth, FL: Sunday Publications, 1984, 140 p.

MACKIN, Theodore. *Divorce and Remarriage*. New York: Paulist Press, 1983, 565 p.

NOONAN, John T. *Power to Dissolve: Lawyers and Marriages in the Courts of the Roman Curia*. Cambridge, MA: The Belkap Press, 1972, 489 p.

ORSY, Ladislas. *Marriage in Canon Law*. Wilmington, DE: Michael Glazier, 1986, 328 p.

SIEGLE, Bernard A. *Marriage According to the New Code of Canon Law*. New York: Alba House, 1986, 297 p.

SPENCE, James R. *Consent to Marriage in a Crisis of Personality Disorder*. Rome: Pont. Greg. Univ., 1985, 102 p.

WRENN, Lawrence G. *Annulments* (5th Revised Edition). Washington, D.C.: C.L.S.A., 1988, 174 p.

WRENN, Lawrence G. *Decisions*. (2nd Edition), C.L.S.A., 1983, 200 p.

WRENN, Lawrence G. *Procedures*. C.L.S.A., 1987, 140 p.

ZWACK, Joseph P. *Annulment: Your Chance to Remarry Within the Catholic Church*. New York: Harper and Row, 1983, 129 p.

ARTICLES

BERNARD, Jean. "The Evolution of Matrimonial Jurisprudence: The Opinion of a French Canonist," in *The Jurist*, XLI (1981), pp. 105-116.

BERNARD, Jean. "The New Matrimonial Law," in *Concilium*, Vol. 185 (1986), pp. 45-53.

BURKE, John J. "The Defender of the Bond in the New Code," in *The Jurist*, XLV (1985), pp. 210-229.

BURKE, Raymond L. "Lack of Discretion of Judgment: Canonical Doctrine and Legislation," in *The Jurist*, XLV (1985), pp. 171-209.

BURKE, Raymond L. and FELLHAUER, David E. "Canon 1095 Canonical Doctrine and Jurisprudence," in *Canon Law Society of America*. Proceedings of the 48th Annual Convention, Washington, DC, C.L.S.A., 1987, pp. 94-117.

BURNS, Dennis J. "The Sacrament of Marriage," in *Chicago Studies* 23 (1984), [The Revised Law of the Church: A Pastoral Guide], pp. 63-76.

COLEMAN, Gerald D. "Can a Person with AIDS Marry in the Church," in *The Jurist*, XLIX (1989), pp. 258-266.

CUNEO, J. James. "Lack of Due Discretion: The Judge as Expert," in *The Jurist*, XLII (1982), pp. 141-163.

CUNEO, J. James. "Deceit/Error of Person as a *Caput Nullitatis*," in Canon Law Society of America, *Proceedings of the 45th Convention* (1987), pp. 154-166.

CUNEO, J. James. "Toward Understanding Conformity of Two Sentences of Nullity," in *The Jurist*, XLVI (1986), pp. 568-601.

CUSCHIERI, Andrew. "*Bonum Coniugum* (c. 1055, 1) and *Incapacitas Contrahendi* (c. 1095, 2-3) in the New Code of Canon Law," in *Monitor Ecclesiasticus*, CVIII (1983), pp. 334-347.

DE LUCA, Luigi. "The New Law on Marriage," in *The New Code of Canon Law: 5th International Congress of*

*Canon Law*, Vol. II, St. Paul Univ., Ottawa (1984), pp. 827-851.

DILLON, Edward J. "Confidentiality in Tribunals," in Canon Law Society of America, *Proceedings of the 45th Convention* (1984), pp. 171-181.

DOYLE, Thomas P. "Matrimonial Jurisprudence in the United States," in *Marriage Studies II: Reflections in Canon Law and Theology*, Catholic Univ. of America (1982), pp. 111-158.

DOYLE, Thomas P. "Marriage," (cc. 1055-1165), in *The Code of Canon Law; A Test and Commentary*, NY: Paulist Press, (1985), pp. 737-833.

EGAN, Edward. "Two Centuries of Experiment and Reform," in Canon Law Society of America, *Proceedings of the 43rd Convention* (1982), pp. 132-144.

EGAN, Edward. "The Nullity of Marriage for Reason of Insanity or Lack of Due Discretion of Judgment," in *E.I.C.*, 1-11 (1983), pp. 9-54.

FELICI, P. "Juridical Formalities and Evaluation of Evidence in the Canonical Process," in *The Jurist*, XXXVIII (1978), pp. 153-157.

FELLHAUER, David E. "Psychological Incapacity for Marriage in the Revised Code of Canon Law," in *The New Code of Canon Law: 5th International Congress of Canon Law*, Vol. II, Ottawa: St. Paul Univ. (1984), pp. 1019-1040.

GALLAGHER, Clarence. "Marriage and the Revised Canon Law for the Eastern Catholic Churches," in *Studia Canonica*, 24 (1990), pp. 69-90.

GRAHAM, John J. "Transsexualism and the Capacity to Enter Marriage," in *The Jurist*, XLI (1981), pp. 117-154.

GRAMUNT, Ignatius and WAUCK, Leroy. "Capacity and Incapacity to Contract Marriage," in *Studia Canonica*, 22 (1988), pp. 147-168.

GRAMUNT, Ignatius. "The Essence of Marriage and the Code of Canon Law," in *Studia Canonica*, 25 (1991), pp. 365-384.

GROCHOLEWSKI, Zenon. "The Ecclesiastical Judge and the Findings of Psychiatric and Psychological Experts," in *The Jurist*, XLVII (1987), pp. 449-470.

GUIRY, Robert W. "Canonical and Psychological Reflections on the *Vetitum* in Today's Tribunal," in *The Jurist*, XLIX (1989), pp. 191-209.

GUIRY, Robert W. "Immaturity, Maturity, and Christian Marriage," in *Studia Canonica*, 25 (1991), pp. 93-114.

HANNON, James I. "The Role of Diagnosis in the Annulment Evaluation Process," in *The Jurist*, XLIX (1989), pp. 182-190.

HENNESSY, Patrick. "Canon 1097: A Requiem for *Error Redundans*?" in *The Jurist*, XLIX (1989), pp. 146-181.

HIMES, Michael J. "The Intrinsic Sacramentality of Marriage: The Theological Ground for the Inseparability of Validity and Sacramentality in Marriage," in *The Jurist*, L (1990), pp. 198-220.

JOHNSON, John G. "Publish and Be Damned: The Dilemma of Implementing the Canons on Publishing the Acts and the Sentence," in *The Jurist*, XLIX (1989), pp. 210-240.

JOHNSON, John G. "Total Simulation in Recent Rotal Jurisprudence," in *Studia Canonica*, 24 (1990), pp. 383-426.

KENNY, Walter F. "Tribunals of Second Instance: The New
York Model Interdiocesan Tribunal," in Canon Law
Society of America, *Proceedings of the 48th Annual
Convention*, Washington, D.C. (1987), pp. 143-145.

LUCAS, John P. "The Prohibition Imposed by a Tribunal: Law,
Practice, Future Development," in *The Jurist*, XLV
(1985), pp. 588-617.

Mc GRATH, Aidan. "On the Gravity of Causes of a Psychologi-
cal Nature in the Proof of Inability to Assume the
Essential Obligations of Marriage," in *Studia
Canonica*, 22 (1988), pp. 67-75.

Mc GUCKIN, Robert M. "The Respondent's Rights in a Matrimonial Nullity Case," in *Studia Canonica*, 18 (1984),
pp. 457-481.

MENDONCA, Augustine. "Antisocial Personality and Nullity of
Marriage," in *Studia Canonica*, 15 (1981), pp. 45-72.

MENDONCA, Augustine. "Schizophrenia and Nullity of
Marriage," in *Studia Canonica*, 17 (1983), pp. 197-
237.

MENDONCA, Augustine. "The Effect of Paranoid Personality
Disorder on Matrimonial Consent," in *Studia
Canonica*, 18 (1984), pp. 253-289.

MENDONCA, Augustine. "The Incapacity to Contract Marriage: Canon 1095," in *Studia Canonica*, 19 (1985),
pp. 260-325.

MENDONCA, Augustine. "The Effects of Personality Disorders
on Matrimonial Consent," in *Studia Canonica*, 21
(1987), pp. 67-123.

MORAN, Thomas A. "Canon 1095, 3 and Post-Traumatic Stress
Disorder," (Unpublished J.C.L. Dissertation), Catholic University of America, Washington, D.C., May
1986.

ORSY, Ladislas. "Matrimonial Consent in the New Code: Glossae on Canons 1057, 1095-1103, 1107," in *The Jurist*, XLIII (1983), pp. 29-68.

PETER, Valentine J. "Judges Must Judge Justly," in *The Jurist*, XLIII (1983), pp. 164-178.

RINERE, Elissa. "Marriage Tribunals — The Mystery Ministry," in Canon Law Society of America, *Proceedings of the 50th Annual Convention*, Washington, D.C. (1988), pp. 181-195.

REIFENBERT, Phillip. "The Revised Code on Proofs in Marriage Nullity Cases: An Overview," in *The Jurist*, XLIII (1983), pp. 237-245.

SANSON, Robert J. "Elements of a Good Sentence," in Canon Law Society of America, *Proceedings of the 50th Annual Convention*, Washington, D.C. (1988), pp. 106-127.

SANSON, Robert J. "Implied Simulation: Grounds for Annulment," in *The Jurist*, XLVII (1988), pp. 747-770.

SKILLIN, Harmon D. "Officials of the Tribunal: Terminology, Qualification, Responsibility," in Canon Law Society of America, *Proceedings of the 45th Annual Convention*, Washington, D.C. (1984), pp. 49-62.

SKILLIN, Harmon D. "Marriage in the Year 2000: A Canonical Perspective," in Canon Law Society of America, *Proceedings of the 52nd Annual Convention*, Washington, D.C. (1990), pp. 36-46.

SUMNER, Philip. "*Dolus* as a Ground for Nullity of Marriage," in *Studia Canonica*, 14 (1980), pp. 171-194.

THUMAS, Paul K. "Marriage Annulments for Gay Men and Lesbian Women: New Canonical and Psychological Insights," in *The Jurist*, XLII (1983), pp. 318-342.

VANN, Kevin W. "*Dolus*: Canon 1098 of the Revised Code of Canon Law," in *The Jurist*, XLVII (1987), pp. 371-393.

WALSH, Maurice B. "The Tribunal and Alcoholics Anonymous," in *The Jurist*, XLIX (1989), pp. 266-272.

WOESTMAN, William H. "Judges and the Incapacity to Assume the Essential Obligations of Marriage, in *Studia Canonica*, 21 (1987), pp. 315-323.

WOESTMAN, William H. "Too Many Invalid Marriages," in *Studia Canonica*, 24 (1990), pp. 193-204.

WRENN, Lawrence G. "Processes," (cc. 1400-1752) in *The Code of Canon Law: A Text and Commentary*, New York: Paulist Press (1985), pp. 945-1045.

WRENN, Lawrence G. "In Search of a Balanced Procedural Law for Marriage Nullity Cases," in *The Jurist*, XLVI (1986), pp. 602-623.

WRENN, Lawrence G. "Refining the Essence of Marriage," in Canon Law Society of America, *Proceedings of the 48th Annual Convention*, Washington, D.C. (1987), pp. 12-28.

ZUZY, James B. "Matrimonial Consent and Immaturity," in *Studia Canonica*, 15 (1981), pp. 199-239.

CHURCH DOCUMENTS

JOHN PAUL II. Apostolic Constitution, "The Christian Family in the Modern World" (*Familiaris Consortio*), November 22, 1981 in *Vatican II: More Post-Conciliar Documents*, Grand Rapids, MI: Eerdmans, 1983, pp. 815-898.

JOHN PAUL II. Address to the Sacred Roman Rota ("Truth in the Service of Justice: Moral Certainty"), February 4, 1980 in C.L.D., IX, pp. 933-941

JOHN PAUL II. Address to the Sacred Roman Rota ("Protection of the Good of the Family"), January 24, 1981, in C.L.D., IX, pp. 941-948.

JOHN PAUL II. "Address to the Sacred Roman Rota: February 5, 1987," in *The Pope Speaks*, Vol. 32 (1987), pp. 131-136.

JOHN PAUL II. Address to the Sacred Roman Rota ("Defender of the Bond"), January 26, 1988 in *The Pope Speaks*, Vol. 33 (1988), pp. 156-160.

JOHN PAUL II. Address to the Sacred Roman Rota ("The Right of Defense"), January 26, 1989 in *The Pope Speaks*, Vol. 34 (1989), pp. 242-245.

PAUL VI. "Encyclical Letter on the Regulation of Births" (*Humanae Vitae*), July 25, 1968 in *Vatican II: More Post-Conciliar Documents*, Grand Rapids, MI: Eerdmans, 1983, pp. 505-509.

VATICAN COUNCIL II. "Pastoral Constitution on the Church in the Modern World" (*Gaudium et Spes*), December 7, 1965, in *Documents of Vatican II*, Austin Flannery, Ed., Boston, MA: St. Paul Editions, 1988, #47-53.

PSYCHOLOGICAL WORKS

AMERICAN PSYCHIATRIC ASSOCIATION. *Diagnostic and Statistical Manual of Mental Disorders* [DSM-III-R]. Washington, D.C.: A.P.A., 1987, 565 p.

HOROWITZ, Mardi J. *Introduction to Psychodynamics*. New York: Basic Books, Inc., 1988, 252 p.

MASTERSON, James F. *The Narcissistic and Borderline Disorders*. New York: Brunner/Mazel, Inc., 1981, 246 pp.

MASTERSON, James F. *The Search for the Real Self: Unmasking the Personality Disorders of Our Age*. New York: The Free Press, 1988, 244 p.

MEHR, Joseph. *Abnormal Psychology*. New York: Holt, Rinehart, and Winston, 1983, 595 p.

NORWOOD, Robin. *Women Who Love Too Much*. New York: St. Martins Press, 1985, 266 p.

RUSSELL, Diana. *The Secret Trauma: Incest in the Lives of Girls and Women*. New York: Basic Books, Inc., 1986, 426 p.

SARASON, I. and SARASON, B. *Abnormal Psychology: The Problem of Maladaptive Behavior*, 4th Ed., Englewood Cliffs, NJ: Prentice Hall, Inc., 1984, 557 p.

SPITZER, R. et al. *A Psychiatrist's Casebook*. New York: Warner Books, 1981, 373 p.

WEISSBERG, Michael. *Dangerous Secrets: Maladaptive Responses to Stress* (Alcoholism, Child Abuse, Incest, Spouse Abuse, Suicide). New York: W.W. Norton and Co., 1983, 266 p.

ST PAULS

This book was designed and published by St. Pauls/Alba House, the publishing arm of the Society of St. Paul, an international religious congregation of priests and brothers dedicated to serving the Church through the communications media. For information regarding this and associated ministries of the Pauline Family of Congregations, write to the Vocation Director, Society of St. Paul, 7050 Pinehurst, Dearborn, Michigan 48126. Phone (313) 582-3798 or check our internet site, www.albahouse.org